PROHIBITION

~ IN ~

CAPE MAY COUNTY

PROHIBITION

— IN —

CAPE MAY COUNTY

WETTER THAN THE ATLANTIC

RAYMOND REBMANN

THE
History
PRESS

Published by The History Press
Charleston, SC
www.historypress.com

First published 2019

Manufactured in the United States

ISBN 9781467140836

Library of Congress Control Number: 2019939740

Notice: The information in this book is true and complete to the best of our knowledge. It is offered without guarantee on the part of the author or The History Press. The author and The History Press disclaim all liability in connection with the use of this book.

Contents

Introduction

Historians claim objectivity for their work. No matter how sincere that belief, subjectivity shows in the selection, arrangement and emphasis of materials used. Decisions made by authors reflect personal visions of subjects.

I'm not a professional historian. I'm an amateur, with a more than casual interest in topics touched upon in this work: Cape May County, my home since 1977, the Prohibition era and alcohol, specifically beer.

I volunteer at a museum located in Dennisville. The town itself is a museum, listed in the National Register of Historic Places. In fact, I coauthored an Arcadia book about the area's history.

While researching that book, I found a photo showing a group of men proudly posing in front of a large mechanical device, a still. The photo was taken not far from where I sat at the museum. The image generated lively discussion and considerable interest in the era in which it was taken. The 1920s. Prohibition.

In checking further, I learned that no one had published a book about how Prohibition affected Cape May County.

I start the book with two short chapters, one a summarized history of pre-Prohibition, the other a history of Cape May County. Both are brief due to size limitations for the book. I refer readers interested in more details about either topic to books listed in the bibliography, especially Daniel Okrent's *Last Call* and Jeffrey Dorwart's *Cape May County, New Jersey*.

As for the alcohol connection, I'm a dedicated home brewer, much like moonshiners of the Jazz Age. Only I do it legally. My workshop in the woods is filled with chillers and flasks, bubbling with yeasts and malts and hops. The counter tops groan under the weight of fermenters filled with beer in various stages of becoming.

I typically have a five-gallon batch brewing, using whatever ingredients are available.

I learned while doing this book that home brewing was illegal in the United States until 1979, when Jimmy Carter, a nondrinker, lifted the ban.

So, for many of us, Prohibition really ended then.

I want to thank two people who helped this book happen. My friend, Mark Herron devoted hours combing through microfilm of old newspapers at the Cape May County Library, finding hundreds of articles that form the basis of this book.

I also want to thank the Friends of Dennis Township Old School House Museum for helping me to research the book at the museum and for brainstorming with me during the process. I'm also thankful for support from a grant awarded to the Friends by Cape May County Culture and Heritage through funds from the NJ Historical Commission, used to help promote the book through local venues.

And, of course, I thank my wife, Alicia, who put up with piles of paper and my obsession with a bygone era. She still tolerates my ongoing quest to brew the perfect beer.

Before Prohibition

In 1830, average consumption of hard liquor in America was 7.1 gallons, compared to today's 2.1 gallons, according to historian W.J. Rorabaugh, explaining America's well-deserved title of "drunkest nation on Earth."

Ten years after Pilgrims force-landed at Plymouth because they'd run out of beer, Puritans arrived aboard a well-stocked fleet of eleven ships, carrying seven hundred settlers, livestock and "necessaries." Among the supplies deemed essential to bring civilization to the wilderness, according to Rorabaugh, were 10,000 gallons of beer and 120 casks of malt to transform into beer once the Puritans were sufficiently settled to build a brewery.

Each settler was provided with casks of wheat, rye and barley seed, essential ingredients for bread, both baked and brewed. Contrary to popular misconceptions of Puritans, they were not opposed to the use of alcohol.

"Drink is in itself a good creature of God," Increase Mather wrote. "To be received with thankfulness. But the abuse of drink is from Satan."

Mather's words may summarize the long-running tension between drink and drunkenness that inspired Americans to create both the saloon and the movement that fought to abolish it. The former evolved from colonial-era inns, mandated by law in places like Massachusetts, where each town was required to have a tavern, one that served beer.

In 1810, breweries produced 6 million gallons of beer. By midcentury, that figure had more than tripled, largely because of the arrival of sizable numbers of Irish and German immigrants. German immigrants introduced

America to a new brew sensation: lager. By 1890, Americans swilled over 850 million gallons of the stuff annually.

The federal government noticed the flood at the taps, seeing untapped revenue. Taxing beer at a dollar a barrel, the federal government quickly generated one-fourth of its annual budget by the end of the nineteenth century.

Brewers didn't complain. The tax gave their industry a certain respectability. Beer became such an accepted product that even the government benefitted from drinking. And with rapid improvements to brewing technology and mass transportation, golden lager flowing from brewers' vats continuously increased the gold flowing into brewers' coffers.

But Americans' drinking habits didn't go unnoticed or unopposed. In the nineteenth century, Protestant clergy and businessmen led a countermovement encouraging temperance. In 1826, the American Temperance Society made its first appearance. Its first decade saw enlistments of over one million members in seven thousand local affiliates.

Their strongest objection was against the saloon, commonly seen mostly in urban areas, beginning in the 1840s. When those European immigrants arrived, many settled in cities. The saloon was an important cultural and social institution for immigrants. A meeting place, a place to conduct business, learn the news and weigh in on important political issues, all of these were functions of the saloon as much as serving drink.

The legal tide turned against saloons in 1913, when Congress passed the Sixteenth Amendment, creating the income tax. With a new source of revenue, the federal government no longer depended upon taxed alcohol to pay its bills. That change gave anti-alcohol groups like the Woman's Christian Temperance Union and Anti-Saloon League an opening to change America's drinking habits by legally banning alcohol.

Pushed by WCTU and ASL, local option law battles raged like brush fires, drying up bits and pieces of the country as relentless prohibitionists fought to ban not just the saloon that served drink, but drink itself. By 1903, one third of America lived under some form of prohibition. By 1913, forty-six million, or half the population, were impacted.

Still the ASL persisted, raising large sums for publicity and state by state political campaigning. In 1914, booze was illegal in fourteen states.

War in Europe provided the final push needed.

In 1916, the *New York World* published evidence that the German-American Alliance, heavily funded by brewers, supported the Kaiser's war effort. "Liquor is the financier of the German Alliance," Wayne Wheeler, ASL head spinmeister, pronounced. "Its purpose is to secure German solidarity."

The enemies of liquor enlisted patriotism in their crusade.

By the time the United States entered World War I in 1917, twenty-six states had gone dry. Nine others banned booze during the war.

Congress passed the Lever Food and Fuel Control Act, which disallowed distilled foodstuffs during wartime. Also impacted, brewers saw grain supplies reduced by 50 percent. Close to an outright ban but not enough to satisfy their dry adversaries.

They'd tried passing prohibition legislation before, falling short in 1876 and 1914. This time, with war-fueled patriotism working in its favor, the ASL launched its final assault on demon rum, an amendment to the constitution mandating national Prohibition.

Congress passed the Eighteenth Amendment on December 18, 1917, and ratification happened quickly. By January 16, 1919, Prohibition was the law of the land.

Brief History of the County

Nearly forty miles of Atlantic coast from Great Egg Inlet in the north to Cape May Point at the mouth of Delaware Bay. Acres of meadow and marsh and woodland. Sand beaches and barrier islands. Thick cedar forest and undulating salt grass. Sluggish streams and turbulent inlets.

Cape May County. Before Henry Hudson spotted it as he passed along the coast, the place was home to a branch of the Delaware tribe, the Lenape. They left the area after their last chief, Nummy, died and was buried somewhere out among the barrier islands.

Permanent white settlers first appeared near the end of the seventeenth century. Men named Hand and Townsend, Leaming and Spicer, Ludlam and Howland. Quakers and Baptists and Presbyterians settled respectively in the upper, middle and lower sections of the peninsula. Some came to find greater religious freedom. Others came for the fishing and whaling.

Self-sufficient pioneers, when they exhausted the whales, they branched out into farming. They hunted and fished for smaller species. They cut the dense woodlands, turning forests into homesteads and trees into exportable lumber.

In those early years, thirty-five families owned 70 percent of the county, according to Rutgers historian Jeffrey Dorwart. They accumulated 79 percent of the livestock and controlled 74 percent of shipping. They dominated local government, holding all the important offices, including sheriff, clerk and surrogate. They controlled the county's few roads, the first created in 1707—typically cutting those roads through wilderness themselves. They

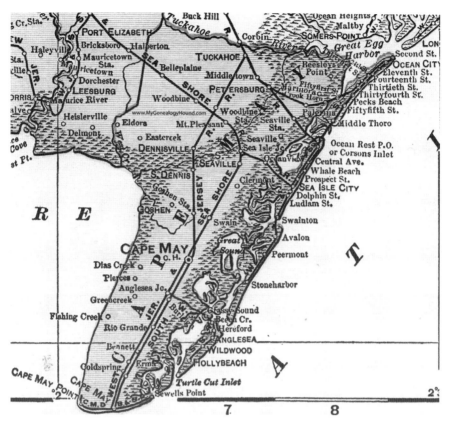

Artist's map of Cape May County. *Dennis Township Museum.*

were the judges, preachers and militia officers. Intermarriage established interlocking kinships, connecting these families. A small group maintained control well after the Revolution.

Land travel was difficult in the early years. Contact with the outside world was made by water, along the Atlantic coast to New York, up Delaware Bay to Philadelphia. The Great Cedar Swamp effectively cut off the southern portion of the peninsula from overland travelers.

Shipbuilding became a major industry. However, no single center dominated. Small communities of shipbuilders thrived near bayside creeks at places like Fishing Creek, Goshen, Dennis Creek and East Creek.

All the while, the county's ocean coast, a necklace of sandy barrier islands, separated by treacherous inlets, remained unpopulated.

WCTU gathering at South Seaville Methodist Camp. *Dennis Township Museum.*

In the first half of the nineteenth century, steamboats enabled traveling Philadelphians to reach the southernmost tip of the peninsula in two days. Cape Island (later renamed Cape May) blossomed into America's first seashore resort. A seven-hundred-room hotel was built in the 1830s by Richard Smith Ludlam, a descendant of several of those first families.

The county remained insulated and isolated through the mid-nineteenth century. Census information from the 1850s shows that 80 percent of the population was born in the county, descended from Anglo-Irish stock.

Rail service arrived after the Civil War. Trains ran to South Seaville, which served as terminal for stage connections to Dennisville, Beeseley's Point, Goshen and Townsend's Inlet.

No large metropolises developed in the county. Residents continued relying upon farming and small, domestic industries. But the railroad would change the area's demographics and economy. Tourists were now able to easily access the area in significant numbers.

One result? The development of the barrier islands as seasonal resorts.

By 1884, train lines extended to the barrier islands, connecting at Sea Isle City and Ocean City. The latter was founded in 1879 by the Lake Brothers, a group including four Methodist ministers. Ocean City was a dry resort. "No spirituous malt intoxications or vinous liquors shall be manufactured, bought, sold, or kept for sale as a beverage on these premises," read deed restrictions applied to building lot purchases by the Ocean City Association.

Methodism, which swept the country in the mid-nineteenth century, brought more change. The original three religious groups who founded the county accommodated a dozen churches built in communities during a burst of Methodist fervor.

The surge wasn't just churches. Methodist camps sprouted in rural areas, offering resort-like settings and an alternative to more secular resorts developing on the barrier islands. One such camp meeting was established at South Seaville in 1865.

The camps were dry communities. First Friday of camp meeting was designated Temperance Day, with activities led by local preachers and leading dry figures such as Captain Samuel Young, "the shouting Methodist."

Camp also offered educational programs for young people, teaching the evils of drink. One rhyming lesson taught children, "Never a glass of cider pour/unless you want it more and more."

Members of prominent local families organized activities. One, Elizabeth Swain, was also president of the county chapter of WCTU. In fact, the WCTU owned its own cottage at South Seaville until 1940.

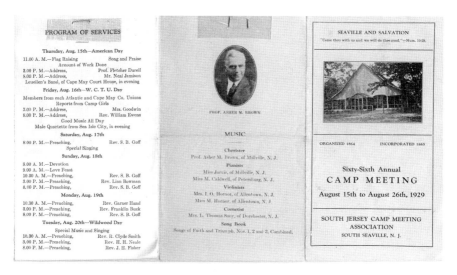

Pamphlet from 1929 Methodist camp meeting at South Seaville. *Dennis Township Museum.*

Cold Spring Inlet, Cape May to the left. *Mark Herron.*

A very different kind of resort took shape on Five Mile Beach.

Late into the nineteenth century, the island was considered "inaccessible and uninhabitable." The only road was an Indian trail overgrown with dense forest and vines.

Enter Phillip Pontius Baker, real estate developer. Baker purchased one hundred acres, calling it the Wildwood Beach Improvement Company.

Clearing building lots and laying out streets, Baker created Holly Beach, with twenty homes and a population of two hundred by 1885.

As the center of the island developed, Baker set his sights on the south end. He filled in marsh and, by 1910, eventually filled Turtle Gut Mile Inlet. Wildwood Crest was incorporated as a borough with Baker as its first mayor.

In 1895, Wildwood was incorporated with Latimer, Baker's brother, as its first mayor.

Holly Beach and Wildwood grew into each other until 1912, when the City of Wildwood was incorporated. One of its first governmental acts was to ban liquor establishments within two hundred feet of the new boardwalk.

Apparently, visitors to the Wildwoods were decidedly wet, because a speakeasy immediately opened in violation of that law, operating at a bathhouse near that boardwalk. Tourists were determined to have their drink, and local entrepreneurs were determined to provide it. Officials perceived their dilemma.

"Let it go and grow or keep it dry and die."

Growth won.

Hotels served alcohol every day, including Sundays, until 1913, when County Prosecutor Matthew Jefferson threatened to arrest Sunday closing law violators. Open bar advocates battled constantly with temperance forces. In 1916 elections, one candidate advocated "liberal" Sunday laws. Opposition organized against not only Sunday booze but also other "vices," including showing "daring" movies and bowling alleys operating on Sunday.

In the winter of 1918–19, the federal government exercised the War Powers Prohibition Act to close saloons within a five-mile radius of Cape May Naval Station. Bar owners and politicians howled, but there was a war on after all.

Little did they know, but this was just a warm-up. The following year, the Volstead Act was enacted.

1920

A new decade. January started a new millennium in America…at least in the minds of some.

The dawn of the Dry Age.

Instead of popping champagne corks and raucous party noise, the mood was solemn and patriotic, as were the settings for New Year celebrations themed "demise of John Barleycorn."

The Woman's Christian Temperance Union had cause to celebrate. After nearly half a century of fighting to end America's enslavement to alcohol addiction, government-mandated Prohibition was now the law of the land.

First Baptist Church of Cape May hosted special services on January 15 to "praise God for victory over rum." Bells chimed, marking the occasion.

Recitations, readings and prayer. Addresses to the faithful from a veritable ecumenical council of clergymen: Curtis Gosserson (First Presbyterian), Herman Pott (First Methodist), P.V. Slaughter (First Baptist). They were joined by Priscilla Rutherford, Cape May's WCTU chapter president, and the venerable Edgar Page Stites, composer of "Beulah Land" and other celebrated hymns.

Wildwood's Francis Downing WCTU chapter conducted a "victory watch" at the Presbyterian church, a songfest of temperance music, peppered with patriotic and inspirational addresses. H.C. Chalmers, supervising principal of county schools, held forth on the Constitution, "its ideals and principles." Reverend C.W. Reamer, Anglesea Methodist Episcopal pastor, spoke on the "18th amendment and how it was adopted." County pastors extolled their flocks on "Righteousness Exalteth a Nation."

Cape May Court House and Goshen faithful gathered in Goshen to hear William F. Daniels, Reverend Thomas Martin and Jennie Wales. Mrs. Ludlam Hand, scion of the second-oldest family in the county, recited a poem. The throng moved to Court House the following night to hear Reverend J.W. Wainwright expound on "law enforcement when and how."

Alfred Cooper's *Cape May Gazette* editorialized John Barleycorn's "last fight" on January 3. "A new American generation will grow up," Cooper wrote, "knowing nothing of the seductiveness, the fascination, or the evils of alcoholic stimulants."

The *Gazette* sounded confident Prohibition would clean up the cities, with money wasted previously at the saloon redirected toward creating better streets, parks and homes. "Prohibition is not a panacea or cure-all for all human ills. Its coming marks a far-reaching step in the efforts of the world's great first democracy to improve conditions under which its people live."

He offered an admonition to diehard wets: "Prohibition is the will and intent of the American people."

That's how the first month of Volstead ended in Cape May County.

The *Philadelphia Inquirer* threw a wet blanket on the celebration with its January 16 report about probable cost of living increases attributable to anticipated federal revenue loss with elimination of the "booze tax." Local tax increases of up to 400 percent were projected.

Children pose at South Seaville Methodist Camp. *Dennis Township Museum.*

Meanwhile, the U.S. Navy spoiled plans of aspiring rumrunners. Commander J.R. Robnett, in charge of selling surplus naval equipment, nixed a bid from certain "unnamed capitalists" hoping to purchase five of the navy's five hundred surplus hydroplanes.

According to the January 24 *Inquirer*, the navy's denial meant there would be none of those "liquid delectables that became taboo with the Volstead Act and the Saharateenth of January last."

The lawbreakers planned to station a well-stocked steamship three miles off Cape May. Planes would collect patrons and fly them to the "oasis" where, according to an apparently overwrought reporter, "they could get soused with a nifty bunk to tumble into when they were stewed in the mode now gone blooey."

"Nothing doing," Robnett informed would-be entrepreneurs. The U.S. Navy wouldn't help the "moonshine gang."

But those imaginative businessmen didn't give up. "Maybe we'll build a light ship and carry out our purpose anyway," an unidentified source told the *Inquirer*.

There was more bad news for New Jersey dries during the second month of Prohibition. The state senate failed to pass the Eighteenth Amendment after the assembly passed it. One senator praised the action, stating that adoption would send a message that New Jersey had been "belted, saddled, and spurred by the Anti-Saloon League."

But there was also a legislative victory for "cold water ranks" when the Senate repealed another bill passed by the assembly that allowed 3.5 percent beer.

Enforcement of the law was the underlying cause of legislators' disagreement, according to Assemblywoman Jennie Van Ness. No trial by jury or provision of search and seizure without warrant were issues that would return to haunt legislators.

It didn't matter what legislation passed—it was likely to be vetoed by the governor, Edward Edwards.

Here's a glimpse at his thinking: "The ASL has, by chicanery, trickery, oppression, and political manipulation forced into the law of this land a so-called amendment to the constitution."

Edwards established himself as a darling of the wets. There was talk of the Democrat running for president. He took aim at Democratic Party icon William Jennings Bryan, denigrating Bryan as a "paid agent of the Anti-Saloon League."

"Nothing under the sun can prevent the 18th amendment from being the outstanding issue in the [upcoming] presidential campaign," Edwards declared, without declaring his candidacy.

Big-city politicians might have been anxious about the loss of booze revenue, but Prohibition already proved to be a "big boon" to Cape May, according to the *Philadelphia North American*. The newspaper proclaimed Volstead to be "working wonders."

Not a single arrest for intoxication. "Booze cases no longer appear on my docket," Judge Henry Eldredge noted.

Business was better than ever. Bank deposits in savings accounts, money that apparently used to fly across saloon bars, grew increasingly robust. Even "farm boys" who formerly "congregated at the local hotel to squander their money on liquor, carried enviable accounts and held shares in the stock market."

As for the class of tourist clientele visiting the area? Innkeepers reported a more "desirable family element of patronage." They were able to charge higher prices to boot.

Some local businesses were probably happy for that additional income in August, after county detectives raided cabarets, pool rooms and soda pop dispensers, finding illegal liquor aplenty. The heretofore idle Judge Eldredge found his workload suddenly increased.

Hotel Germantown North Wildwood. *George F. Boyer Historical Museum.*

Dry agents followed up with raids on Five Mile Beach cafés and hotels. These visits netted an estimated $25,000 in liquid contraband.

Known as Little Mexico of the Jersey shore, alleged miscreants in Anglesea included Hotel Royal, Henry Borbach, proprietor; Inlet Hotel, Robert Moore, proprietor; Bishop's Café, Luke Bishop, proprietor; Germantown Café, William Bishop, proprietor; and Ruric Hotel.

Leading the raids was Reverend R.E. Johnson, pastor of 29th Street Methodist Church of Philadelphia, who doubled as a "secret agent for the Prohibition Enforcement Bureau," according to the *Philadelphia Public Ledger*.

Johnson summered at Anglesea. Knowing all the local dens of iniquity, he led raiders with "coolness." The visit to Moore's was especially profitable, netting $20,000 in wet goods. The raids apparently roused dry forces. The year closed with considerable WCTU activity in the county.

Church services at Cape May Presbyterian featured addresses by Mrs. James Ware, New Jersey superintendent of medical temperance, along with her county version, Elizabeth Swain, leading a celebration of Prohibition's "first anniversary." Similar gatherings took place in Eldora, Goshen and Wildwood. Avalon and Stone Harbor combined meetings and heard Pastor Sara Phillips, scientific temperance instruction superintendent for Pennsylvania, orate on "scientifically proven problems of alcohol."

The county's own scientific temperance instructor, Roxanna Gandy of South Dennis, organized an essay contest for area public schools on the evils of drink.

There was dissent among the dry ranks. Not all clergymen waxed enthusiastic about the new law. Episcopal bishop Paul Matthews addressed a gathering at Wildwood's St. Simeon Church at year's end. According to the *Cape May County Times*, Matthews hurled an "ethical bomb" at legislative efforts by reformers pressing for total abstinence.

"They are like tigers....They've tasted blood and don't know when to stop," Matthews opined, insisting that morality "can not be legislated. It must be molded from within during maturity." As for the Volstead Act, Matthews offered a final thought, "It is the thirstiest proposition I've ever encountered."

Enforcement, education, eradication. It didn't seem to matter. Even before 1920 drew to a close, it was obvious that a glaring loophole weakened the Volstead Act. Consuming alcoholic beverages remained legal. And there were a lot of thirsty people in New Jersey.

A basic law of economics, supply and demand, is remorseless and clear. If there exists a demand, there exists someone who will figure out a way to supply.

1921

The *Philadelphia Inquirer* opened 1921 with a Wildwood story, describing a feat of sleight of hand far surpassing the skills of your two-bit boardwalk carnival huckster.

Booze worth $10,000 disappeared. Supposedly safe under lock and key at Wildwood City Hall, the liquor had been confiscated the previous fall during the raid in Anglesea led by Dr. Johnson. Acting upon instructions from Leo Crossen, their chief in Philadelphia, Prohibition agents descended from Atlantic City. Examining a few sample cases, they discovered that high-octane liquors had been replaced with soda pop.

Further investigation uncovered jugs of gin transformed into fruit juice while 86 proof contents of a fifty-gallon barrel of whisky miraculously transformed to water and vinegar.

Miracle of Cana in reverse.

Of the entire stock of contraband, agents determined that 75 percent had been "substituted." No one at city hall knew anything. The mayor was questioned, but he was eliminated as a suspect, having only recently been restored to high office following a state investigation about "irregularities" surrounding his election. The agents took the remaining liquor to Atlantic City for safekeeping.

The *Pittsburgh Gazette* headline speculated about the identity of the "Wizard of Wildwood." Local cops expressed wide-eyed astonishment when informed of the condition of the cache they'd been watching over so assiduously.

Naturally, local pundits offered suggestions as to the whereabouts of the booze. The *Philadelphia Public Ledger* contributed to that pile, reporting on a rumrunning submarine posing as a lobster boat.

Meanwhile, beachcombing horizon gazers were distracted by the appearance "just offshore" of a commodious houseboat, towed by a barge. Those in the know decided the floating house provided accommodations for whisky runners from the Bahamas who'd recently set up shop off the Jersey coast. A few intrepid swimmers attempted freestyling out to the craft, only to be "rescued" by vigilant Cape May lifeguards.

The Coast Guard took the situation seriously. Manning speedboats disguised as fishing smacks, guardsmen worked in tandem with revenue cutters, cordoning off sections of coastal areas where whisky runners supposedly landed thousands of dollars' worth of booze between Atlantic City and Cape May Point.

Smugglers ran a step ahead of them, using their profits to fit out vessels capable of faster movement to avoid capture and easily navigate the county's many inlets and tidal creeks.

By midsummer, they operated with such impunity that the *Sayre (PA) Evening Times* reported plans for "dotting the Atlantic coast beyond the three-mile limit with floating bars." Liquor vendors supposedly tried buying 287 derelict wooden vessels for that purpose. The alleged seller declined to confirm or deny that report.

According to Roy Haynes, Federal Prohibition commissioner, if rum sellers "are placed under a foreign registry, the government can't touch them."

The Coast Guard had already refused to deploy cutters beyond the three-mile territorial water limit.

Meanwhile, Rum Row took more definite shape.

Locally, the *Star and Wave* reported that two Wildwood men were arrested, but their entire truckload of whisky went missing, having "failed to reach its destination." The county was thrown into a state of "excitement and curiosity."

Spotter planes assisted cutters searching for "mysterious ships" described by newspapers throughout the summer as delivering booze to the beaches, while federal agents hunted for that missing truck, filled with 450 cases of whisky. Cape May County sheriff Meade Tomlin stationed heavily armed deputies and detectives at county bridges. They were instructed to "shoot to kill" drivers of trucks failing to stop when ordered to do so.

The *Star and Wave* pointed out that while all this activity kept dry forces occupied, the county's entire Delaware Bay coast was "wide open for business."

By mid-summer, the rum fleet was in place.

Rum schooner underway. *boatchases.com*.

The *Public Ledger*'s July 23 headline described the Jersey shore as "flooded" with liquor. Opening paragraphs offered details about the fleet's four speedy schooners, "equipped with two 50 horsepower engines," and "twelve thousand cases of Irish and Scotch whisky were brought ashore every month via an armada of fast flying bank boats." Coming out of the Bahamas at sixteen dollars a case, the booze cost four or five times that much by the time it reached thirsty consumers.

The government sprang into action in typical fashion. Both the Coast Guard and Treasury Department launched investigations, both concluding that local ground troops were "ineffective." But the bottom line appeared to be that local enforcement failed to act because no "higher up" had specifically instructed them to act. The brass responded predictably, citing statute book and verse, reminding locals what they already knew: "Importation of alcohol for beverage purposes is illegal and agents were there to enforce the law."

The Coast Guard was more specific, authorizing its units to "inspect for custom all vessels within four leagues of the US coast." Commander Reynolds had more to say: "Cutters may also go to sea after any booze ship even though it's doing business any distance off shore (beyond the limit) and search any vessels which approach said booze ship, take liquor from it and leave it. They may then follow these vessels to within the three-mile limit and seize them."

The navy also pitched in to help.

Rumrunner makes a sale. *Society Page*.

Sixteen navy seaplanes, flying low in battle formation, initiated searches of every bay and inlet on the southern New Jersey coast looking for "whisky caches."

Statements of official determination and displays of firepower surely sufficient to cow even the most determined desperadoes?

Hardly.

The Battle of Rum Row was on.

***

In Cape May County, local attention was distracted by two events seemingly unrelated to the booze brawl brewing offshore.

On October 31, eleven fishermen drowned off Hereford Inlet at Anglesea when their two open boats capsized in that area's treacherous waters. Three bodies were recovered. The men worked for Augustus Hilton, former mayor of Anglesea, Cape May County freeholder, local real estate developer, owner of one of the region's largest fish processing companies.

Hilton expressed dismay that the tragedy had not been prevented, noting the proximity of a lifesaving station overlooking Hereford Inlet. Hilton's allegation of dereliction of duty was investigated by Rudolph Ridgely, inspector of the Fifth District of Life Guards, according to the *New York Times*.

Captain Price defended the men of his station, noting that the "weather was very thick off the coast, making long distance observation impossible."

The fishing season having concluded, Hilton's eleven men were dispatched to the fishing grounds to retrieve poles used to hold their nets. Eight poles, each seventy feet long, were to be brought in, floating alongside the boat. Each weighed about five hundred pounds. Local fishermen observed that even six such poles made "heavy weight even in a smooth sea."

Fishermen added that going out at Hereford in such weather was "foolhardy," especially since the area's most protected inlet at Cold Spring was close at hand. The *Philadelphia Inquirer* reported the coroner's inquiry and jury of six, including three sea captains, ruled the deaths "accidental with no negligence on the part of the lifesaving service."

Gus Hilton was a big man in the county, literally, standing six feet, four inches. He originally settled in Anglesea in 1888 with his first wife, Elizabeth, and a son, John. His second son, Frank, was born in 1891.

Hilton also towered over most other men in the scope of his holdings and his ambitions for the future of Anglesea. He owned the Hotel Hilton

Pole used by fishermen at ready at Otten's Harbor. *George F. Boyer Historical Museum.*

at First Avenue. In addition to starting his Aspen Fish Company (eventually changed to Consolidated Fishing Company), Hilton was a founder of Wildwood Yacht Club, an officer in Five Mile Beach Electric Light and Power Company and in Five Mile Beach Building and Loan Association. He owned a large number of building lots on the island and was committed to Wildwood's continued growth.

While his interests and involvements varied from organizing Anglesea Volunteer Fire Company to helping establish a Methodist church, Hilton had a few scrapes with the law in the operations of his fishing company. He was also arrested for selling liquor at his hotel on Sundays and for keeping illegal slot machines. The latter occurred before Volstead but it evidences a willingness to go beyond the law to get what he wanted.

What he wanted was prosperity—for himself and for his adopted hometown.

In the 1920s in Cape May County, prosperity meant tourists. Tourists demanded easier access to the area. That meant roads. In 1920, 6.7 million traveled in cars on America's roads, almost four times more than in 1915. That figure would quadruple by 1930.

A road to Cape May (Route 9) had been recently completed, making access easier, but more were needed—and existing roads required maintenance. Hilton also figured in the year's other major non-Volstead story, a tale of political corruption.

Hilton served as director for Cape May County Board of Chosen Freeholders, the governing body. The *Bridgewater Courier News* reported on November 22 that Hilton and nine other freeholders, facing malfeasance charges related to the awarding of road contracts, had changed earlier "not guilty" pleas to "no contest."

The issues were freeholder collusion to fix prices on road projects, padding costs of projects, entering into "sweetheart" deals with favored contractors and other accounting "irregularities." The secret of their being able to do it for so long so blatantly? They were all in on it.

Common pleas judge Henry Eldredge heard the case, reluctantly. He'd originally asked that it be moved out of county, fearing inability to secure an unbiased jury. The plea change eliminated that concern. Eldredge assessed fines ranging from $200 to $2,000, with Hilton hit for $500.

While criminal behavior within county government was being disorganized, rum fleet organizing proceeded.

The *Asbury Park Press* reported that international whisky rings, backed by millions of dollars, were setting up along the New Jersey coast—"headquartered not far from Atlantic City."

Steamers heading north from the Bahamas loaded with fifteen to twenty thousand cases joined schooners carrying smaller loads of choice European booze. According to the *Press*, "enterprising locals" got in on the action. Fishermen along the coast "reaped a harvest for their forbidden cargoes." If the prose didn't sound musical to the ear, the profits surely did.

Paid fifteen dollars for each case landed, local watermen didn't resist temptation. Their knowledge of area geography and deserted beaches, best for landing cargoes, was invaluable to smuggling operations.

Convoys of motorized vehicles waited at each landing site. Men quickly unloaded boats and reloaded trucks then whisked the liquid loot off to warehouses secreted in mainland woods and farms.

The feds planned to counter this invasion with a naval "dragnet" of submarines. But there was a problem. Who would pay for it? The Prohibition Bureau budget lacked funds to cover a submarine sandwich let alone a submarine dragnet. Bureau Commissioner Haynes hoped the U.S. Navy would pick up the tab.

Navy brass torpedoed the idea.

The Coast Guard "stood by," waiting to "cooperate with other government forces" to catch the smugglers. Its cutters were ready to go, but the Coast Guard had other duties, including lifesaving, search and rescue and hunting for derelict ships, limiting its ability to fully engage.

Fish processing plant at Otten's Harbor, Wildwood, New Jersey. *George F. Boyer Historical Museum.*

Aerial view of fish processing plant at Richardson's Sound. *George F. Boyer Historical Museum.*

Its major proactive move was to redeploy several vessels from its Pacific theater to beef up the Atlantic.

In short order, these too were standing by.

Enforcement officials did board one vessel, the *Pocomoke*, off Atlantic City. Its paperwork showed the cargo was bound for Canada, so no action was taken. However, some booze was apparently jettisoned off Cape May County, where it made its way into an ill-fated convoy directed by Emmanuel "Manny" Katz.

The *New York Times* described Katz as a "master mind" of a gigantic smuggling combine. And if that didn't keep Katz sufficiently occupied, he also operated the Hotel Whittle in wet, wet Atlantic City.

The mastermind was arrested on July 17 in Cape May County, caught with 152 cases of scotch, which the *Times* reported were "currently stored safely at the county court house, guarded by two armed deputy sheriff."

That haul, law enforcement conceded, was but a small portion of an "immense consignment" landed around Ocean City and Wildwood. Each case bore the same stamp: "Nassau, Bahamas via New York."

Katz's particular consignment had been run up a deep channel between Wildwood and the mainland. The load was brought to a fish "reducing" plant at Richardson Sound. The channel had been dredged to permit fishing vessels to reach the wharf at the plant.

The liquor had come from the Bahamas aboard those same "mysterious ships" that continued to plague authorities. Coast Guard cutters had circled these vessels threateningly but could do no more because they remained outside the three-mile limit. Somehow, carrier boats eluded authorities, managing to land their cargoes.

Katz was arrested by Wildwood officials while he sat at the wheel of a Stutz roadster directing a motorized convoy carrying the 152 cases of booze. That evidence was displayed in Eldredge's courtroom on July 29, along with the two armed deputies guarding it. A crowd of the parched, many obvious Katz partisans, filed into the courtroom.

The *Public Ledger* offered a detailed description of the protagonist: "Dapper, as usual. Well set up and appearing healthy-looking with well-brushed, iron grey hair....Dressed in the meticulous fashion for which he is noted, he bore himself as jauntily as if he hadn't a care in the world."

No word on how the prosecution looked.

Katz sounded pretty bon vivant for a hotelier facing big trouble with the law. He was represented by Robert McClain, former state attorney general, who immediately asked Eldredge to dismiss the case. The judge turned thumbs down.

McClain then motioned for a trial by jury. Under New Jersey's law, Eldredge had that option. He denied the motion.

County Prosecutor Eugene Cole called Wildwood City officials who witnessed and participated in the event to testify. This bevy of Wildwood officialdom included: former mayor W.C. Hendee, Police Chief William Hardy, Justice of the Peace John Byrne, trucking company operators Kenneth Kirby and Richard Coney and City Clerk Alfred Winterburn.

Winterburn testified he'd observed a truck being loaded at Richardson Sound fish plant. He contacted the others. Those officials obtained a "John Doe" warrant before joining the intrepid clerk. Winterburn observed Katz follow the loaded trucks in his roadster.

The "irregular sleuths" followed the convoy, driving nearly the length of the county toward Ocean City. There, the trucks were stopped by two local policemen, who "took possession" of the cargo.

Police Chief Hardy intervened, threatening Katz with arrest, flashing the warrant. Katz challenged his authority to act. Katz pushed Hardy away from the Stutz and sped off. He was eventually arrested in Atlantic City.

Eldredge found Katz guilty of transporting illegal liquor, and he imposed the maximum sentences of a $500 fine and six months' jail time. The *Star and Wave* applauded Eldredge, who'd pledged to "enforce the Van Ness Act in Cape May County and assist federal authorities in breaking up the rum ring."

That evening, McClain reached New Jersey Supreme Court Justice Katzenbach at his Spring Lake summer home. McClain obtained a writ of a certiorari, ordering Katz released on $2,000 bail pending his appeal.

Interviewed by the *New York Times*, Katz complained about being denied a jury trial and intended to "test the constitutionality of the Van Ness Act." Attorney McClain indicated denial of the jury trial was the basis of his client's appeal. "That's not all," Katz continued, indignant about losing 152 cases of good whisky, "when I asked the sheriff for a drink of my own liquor, he refused."

That booze, by the way, was 86 proof, certified by chemists from Philadelphia, brought in by the prosecution. Authorities believed it was part of the haul that made it ashore from *Pocomoke*, a British-flagged schooner taken by authorities to Atlantic City.

Safely returned on bail to friendly Atlantic City, surrounded by his many "friends," Manny offered observations about Cape May County jail: "Not such a bad place. I had ice cream and cake. The sheriff's a bully good fellow who made my stay as pleasant as possible."

But Manny expressed no desire to spend the "torrid days" of summer in a "stuffy jail."

While Katz's appeal was considered, there was no letup in the rum traffic. The Jersey shore was wetter than ever. Local Coast Guardsmen continued to "watch and wait," anticipating orders to spring into action.

Katz's skirmishes with the law were hardly finished. A subsequent *Times* item reported that his "fashionable suburb, Ventnor City" had been raided. Katz was again arrested for violating the Volstead Act.

No ice cream and cake at Cape May County jail this time.

***

Smugglers weren't distracted by the Katz case. In fact, they improved their methods for providing liquor. The *Public Ledger* reported that 369 surplus World War I submarine chasers had been sold off by the government. Many of these wide-hulled, 110-foot boats were converted into speedy craft capable of eighteen knots in rough seas while durable enough to withstand nasty weather and turbulence common in this part of the Atlantic.

The U.S. Customs Service entered the rum war at this point. "There's enough whisky and gin in the West Indies to keep people intoxicated for the next hundred years. It'll take an army the size of the AEF [American Expeditionary Force] to stop smuggling along the Atlantic coast," Special Treasury Agent Nicholas Brooks noted.

What he didn't say was just as obvious. The government didn't get a nickel in tax revenue from sales of the stuff.

Before Prohibition took effect, many of the big liquor dealers dumped their stock on the market, where it was bought and stored internationally, especially in the Bahamas. That booze was now being smuggled into the United States.

Locally, customs officials closely monitored Two Mile Beach, south of Wildwood. A fisherman reported two surf boats had landed casks of whisky that were loaded onto waiting trucks and whisked away. The smugglers had pulled revolvers on the fisherman, holding him captive during the proceedings.

This was part of a rumored "hidden cache" of some five thousand cases at Two Mile, described as "the most desolate stretch on the Jersey coast."

"It's possible for fishing smacks going in and out of Cold Spring Inlet to land hooch at Two Mile without my patrols seeing it," Captain Joseph Springer of the Cape May Coast Guard Station conceded.

The feds reacted to the rumor, swarming around Wildwood and Turtle Gut Inlet, seeking a particular fishing vessel suspected of being involved in the Bahamian trade. They found nothing but resentment from locals.

"Gotten so you can't drop a mud hook without some lubber whispering you're a rumrunner," one old salt groused.

But you didn't have to be Sherlock Holmes to detect those who'd gotten in on the action.

"Ever' body knew what was goin' on," a local recalled, years later. "You knew right off when a man wasn't fishin' and was runnun' rum. First place, his family ate proper and you could tell by what they bought at the grocery store or whether they had to run a grub bill come winter."

It wasn't just fishermen trying to make a buck. The tourist trade needed liquor to keep bottom lines fluid. The summer of 1921 concluded with raids in Wildwood. Among businesses hit were the Inlet Hotel and Royal Hotel in Anglesea and Dew Drop Inn at Otten's Harbor. These businesses and their proprietors, Adam Kosobucki (Royal), George Moore (Inlet) and Louisa

Dew Drop Inn on the waterfront, Otten's Harbor. *George F. Boyer Historical Museum.*

Booth (Dew Drop) would appear in newspapers frequently throughout Prohibition, and Anglesea, Schellenger Avenue and Otten's Harbor were hotbeds of illegal activity.

With the rum war heating up, Governor Edwards declared Prohibition a "flat failure and an instrument of vice and corruption" during an interview in Atlantic City, where he met with state Democratic Party leaders about his prospects for the U.S. Senate.

Edwards claimed enforcers of Volstead were often its "most flagrant violators." He called Prohibition "an infringement upon personal liberty" while stressing he was a nondrinker who was "against the saloon."

"No nation ever became great on a 'thou shalt not' diet."

He also raised the revenue issue, pointing out that bootleggers got rich from funds that formerly went into government treasuries, resulting in tax increases, including personal income. Edwards left no doubt about his prospective Senate run. He was the wet candidate.

By the end of September, federal agents charged the Anglesea-based fishing schooner *A&E Blackman*, owned by Walnut House proprietor Martin Hochesang, with smuggling liquor from the Bahamas. An estimated one thousand cases of booze were confiscated and arrests were made, including the vessel's owner.

Also arrested was U.S. Deputy Collector of Internal Revenue Joseph Schiff in Camden. He was charged with assisting in landing 1,400 cases from the *Blackman* on the Delaware River. The *Blackman* was also involved in criminal activity of another sort: oyster poaching at Maurice River. Or was that ploy, decoying the boat's presence in the area, for more lucrative criminality?

Another non-piscine catch occurred at West Creek Landing on Delaware Bay. A "mysterious tip" directed state troopers to a remote landing where they encountered men unloading five hundred cases from a barge onto horse-drawn wagons. The booze had been transported up the bay to the landing. From there, troopers assumed it would have been carted to the concrete highway (Route 47) then transferred to trucks.

As 1921 drew to a close there was some Keystone Kops comic relief in Wildwood at the Elmira Hotel, formerly the College Inn. Just as a keg of beer was tapped, feds entered, announcing a raid. Thinking it a holiday prank, partiers ignored the agents. The beer flowed.

After agents finally convinced lawbreakers the party was over, bartenders tried concealing untapped kegs, but the agents forced them to empty out all that high-powered brew—and not one drop into an empty glass.

This was not the Elmira's first raid, nor would it be the last. The Elmira's owner, David Kirk, had recently purchased the hotel, but after several scrapes with the law, Kirk had apparently had enough. He abandoned his property and fled the area. The next owner of the Elmira was Charles Bradley, who'd sold the hotel to Kirk but held the mortgage. Bradley owned another hotel nearby, named for himself. He too was well known among Prohibition agents.

The Bradley Hotel was a popular Five Mile Beach café, especially known for catering to traveling salesmen. Bradley was summoned to Trenton to show cause why his business should not be padlocked for liquor violations. Perhaps Bradley hoped to cut a deal because he removed the bar and reopened the business as a restaurant. But it was too little too late to placate state authorities, and Bradley's doors were locked.

Also padlocked at this time was the Hamlet Hotel, directly behind Bradley's. Up in Anglesea, the Inlet and Royal received similar treatment.

The year ended badly for Jennie Van Ness too. Author of the New Jersey Prohibition Enforcement Act, Van Ness ran for reelection but finished last in a field of twelve assembly candidates. And that was the Republican primary.

Pearce Franklin, a wet candidate, won the race.

Van Ness's signature legislation was challenged as well. The state's court of errors and appeals held special sessions to decide the act's constitutionality. The state supreme court had previously upheld the act, but three cases were selected from more than two hundred adjudicated under Van Ness to make a final decision.

One of these was Manny Katz's case.

His attorney, Robert McClain, represented the wet side of the argument. One key legal sticking point was the act's denial of trial by jury. Another was a discrepancy between Volstead's use of the word *crime* in describing illegal acts involving liquor, while Van Ness referred to "disorderly persons."

Legislators on both sides of the aisle prepared amended versions of Van Ness should the court strike down the original.

In other news, the *Evening Courier (Camden)* reported on December 30 about the resignation of Reverend John B. Adams as pastor of Billingsport Methodist Church. A minister since 1909, Adams officially joined the war against demon rum as a federal Prohibition officer. He joined the ranks of a select group known as "Raiding Parsons."

Otherwise, the year ended with New Jersey in liquor limbo.

Model Rumrunner

An August edition of *New Bedford Evening Standard* described one rumrunner carrying five thousand cases of booze valued at $500,000. Costing him $8 per bottle in the Bahamas, and allowing for costs to pay crew and suppliers, each excursion to Rum Row netted Bill McCoy $400,000.

Lawbreakers, especially when the law is unpopular, come up with a "larger than life" character to serve as their antihero. For rumrunners of the Atlantic coast, there was no more likely candidate than Bill McCoy. McCoy is sometimes hailed as founding father of Rum Row. Thumbing his nose at federal agents and Coast Guard skippers, McCoy was the best-known rum captain on the Nassau to New Jersey circuit.

How successful were the rumrunners?

In 1917, Bahamas cleared about 4,000 gallons of liquor. Five years later, near the height of the row's glory, that figure had skyrocketed to 1.3 million gallons. According to McCoy biographer Frederic Van de Walter, McCoy alone supplied over 700,000 cases during his stint on the circuit, before his schooner *Tomoka* was captured by Coast Guard cutter *Seneca* off Sea Bright in 1923.

McCoy's popularity with wet consumers derived from a perception of his honest dealing with customers. He never watered his booze to stretch profits the way competitors did. And he only sold "top shelf" liquor—no doctored substitutes.

He may not have actually been the inspiration for the phrase "the real McCoy," but many satisfied imbibers along the Jersey shore employed it in drinking to his character.

THE REAL McCOY
SCOTCH

Walker Black Label	$22.50
Dewar's Ne Plus Ultra	$21.50
Buchanan's	$20.00
Haig Pinch	$19.00
King William	$16.50
Old Parr	$16.00
Black and White	$13.00
Green Stripe	$13.00
Dewar's White Label	$13.00
Haig Gold Label	$13.00
King George Gold Label	$13.00
Walker Red Label	$13.00
White Horse	$13.00
Sandy McDonald	$12.00
Bullock & Lade Thistle	$12.00
Peter Dawson	$10.00
Bullock & Lade Gold Label	$10.00
Rob Boy	$10.00
Old Mull	$ 9.50
Munroe Square Bottle	$ 9.50
Huntly's Blend	$ 9.50
Strathdon	$ 8.00
Claymore	$ 8.00
Ambassador (24 pts.)	$ 8.50

GIN

Gordon Dry—Frosted bottle	$ 6.50
Burke's Dry	$ 6.00
De Kuyper's Holland	$ 5.25
Booth's High and Dry	$ 6.50
Gordon's Old Tom—Frosted bottle	$ 6.00

INEXPENSIVE QUALITY - The incredible prices of the booze McCoy sold by the case beyond the 12-mile limit.

Menu from the Real McCoy. *The Real McCoy.*

Hold of rumrunner filled with sacks of booze. *static.messynessychic.com.*

McCoy was more than just an honest criminal. He was an innovator.

He developed the "burlock," a pyramid-shaped package holding six bottles. The package was cased in straw for support against rough handling. The burlocks were sewed inside burlap.

He also mastered distribution, never permitting more than two prospective buyers aboard at a given time. Theft prevention measures consisted of a keen-eyed seaman manning a machine gun while shoppers browsed. This system helped McCoy avoid the many hijackings that plagued the row.

His transactions were conducted in cash, preferably large bills. McCoy was paid $60 per case, which in turn sold for $120 per case on land. Prices fluctuated according to supply and demand.

McCoy was one of the first operators to join the row in 1921.

The early years were easier going than later in the decade when the presence of organized crime became more pervasive. McCoy described the row's "society on the water" complete with deliveries of morning newspapers and fresh milk. Nearby fishing boats were always willing to swap fresh fish or lobster "shorts" (undersized) for cases of booze.

McCoy was eventually caught and spent time in federal prison. Upon release, he did not return to Rum Row.

Talking about it in *The Real McCoy*, McCoy said he'd recoiled from the venality that had taken over the trade. McCoy had always considered himself a "true patriot," providing a product to customers unjustly denied their right to purchase.

McCoy died in Florida in 1948, aboard the *Blue Lagoon*, a forty-eight-foot yacht he designed and built. He was seventy-one.

1922

"V an Ness Act Unconstitutional," the *Philadelphia Inquirer* headline trumpeted. New Jersey started 1922 without a state law enforcing Prohibition. The state's court of errors and appeals had reversed the supreme court.

As with many complicated and controversial legal questions, there were differences of opinion among judges, except on the issue of trial by jury, which the state constitution says is "inviolable." Van Ness infringed upon defendants' rights by denying that option, as in the Manny Katz case. Jury trial is a fundamental right of common law guaranteed under state and federal law.

One area of disagreement among judges concerned the degree of violation of Prohibition law. Was the violator guilty of a crime or a disorderly person's offense? Also debated was the issue of who had police powers, state or federal government. The court gave the nod to the federal power. In truth, other issues were rendered moot by the overriding issue of jury trial. On this, the judges primarily based their ruling.

Legislators rushed back to drawing boards to develop a replacement law.

Stories of submarine rumrunners resurfaced in January with the *Trenton Times* reporting a sighting by two fishermen about twenty miles off Cape May, approaching the entrance to Delaware Bay.

The fishermen indicated they were hailed about ten miles out by a "small craft." Its skipper asked for directions to Two Mile Beach. The site of the legendary cache of liquor had apparently grown famous.

Next night, the *Allentown Call* reported, a thirty-foot vessel was sighted with no running lights. Joined by two others, the three pulled close to the beach at Two Mile. A body of men went ashore. One intrepid observer, spying on their activities, reported that the men on shore signaled a "dark grey sub" lurking off Five Fathom Lightship, located twenty miles off shore.

Captain Joe Springer ordered a chaser steamed up and ready to pursue from the nearby Naval Air Station dock, should the mysterious vessel reappear.

New Jersey seemed fated to become the wettest state in the union with only twenty agents to enforce Volstead laws statewide and no reinforcements planned. Prisoners held or awaiting sentencing for violations under the discredited Van Ness Act were released. Prosecutors pledged to continue vigilance, but to what end with no state legal apparatus on which to base actions?

The Anti-Saloon League was busily drafting legislation, the *New York Times* noted. Hopefully, none of those drafts was stored near white mule moonshine.

A half pint of the locally produced booze had been secured as evidence in a safe at the county prosecutor's office. A stack of legal documents was stored alongside. The mule turned "restive" during the night and popped its cork, splashing a miniscule amount onto the paperwork.

Next morning, the documents were riddled with burn holes where the mule had kicked. This came as no surprise to experienced white mule tipplers. There was a ritual for imbibing the stuff, according to an unnamed source living in the woods where the mule originated.

"Take a deep breath and hold. Open the jar and take a big gulp fast. Immediately replace and tighten the lid. Swallow. Hold on to some stable object. Then and only then, attempt to breathe."

Expected side effects include coughing, wheezing, gasping and choking, accompanied by uncontrollable shaking. Near-death experiences were common.

When, or if, stability returned, the drinker wiped streaks of fuel oil residue from his lips and sighed in relief—happy to have survived the mule's kick.

And ready for another pull at the jar.

In 1922, sixty-five-year-old John Peterson from Cape May was found dead in a shack. State police attributed cause of death to overdose of "white mule."

In March, the Coast Guard captured the fifteen-ton schooner *Comanche*, under Captain Theodore Riddle out of Anglesea, but not before the crew tossed a quantity of booze overboard.

The *Five Mile Beach Journal* reported the chase was a "lively affair." The *Comanche* refused to obey numerous hails and headed north along the inland waterway.

Coast Guard captain Samuel Holdzkon, knowing he couldn't match *Comanche*'s speed, commandeered an automobile and chased overland, finally heading off the rumrunner at the Dorset Avenue bridge near Ventnor. There, the *Comanche* again ignored an order to halt and turned around to head south.

Once again the Coast Guard pursued, and nine men squeezed into a single car took up the chase.

This time they commandeered a speedboat. They finally overtook their quarry, firing several revolver shots across the bow. The *Comanche* surrendered, its crew tossing boxes overboard where they quickly sank.

Coast Guardsmen boarded but were unable to find any booze. The captain and crew of the schooner were arrested. No charges were filed. But the intrepid Holdzkon knew where to look for the evidence needed to make a case.

That same week, the *New York Times* declared New Jersey was "getting wet with no dry law." Reacting to either the *Times* swipe or the *Comanche* incident, the Coast Guard stepped up its activity in the rum war, announcing that gunners on cutters had been ordered to "shoot to kill" smugglers attempting to land cargoes after ignoring orders to stop.

"We're tired of being playthings for the rum running syndicate," a spokesman explained. Previous procedure had called for restraint. Gunners used blanks and fired over the heads of the quarries.

The Coast Guard had reason to cheer later in the year. As reported in the *Wilmington Evening Journal*, 375 packages of booze, each containing six-quart bottles of scotch, had been recovered from the cargo the *Comanche* crew had jettisoned in the back bay. More significantly, the alleged owner of the boat, Frank Hilton, had been arrested by state police.

Listed as hailing from Brooklyn, Hilton was actually a home-grown product, son of former Anglesea mayor Augustus Hilton.

Frank was described as "head and brains" behind a large enterprise, "one of the largest whisky smuggling rings in the country." Government officials had been hunting for him for months.

Hilton was turned over to U.S. marshals and taken to Trenton and jailed.

***

Hilton's hometown was a busy place even when rumrunners weren't active. At the south end of the island, Turtle Gut Inlet was filled in 1922, facilitating development while connecting the Wildwoods to Two Mile Island.

Train stop at Grassy Sound before entering Anglesea. *George F. Boyer Historical Museum.*

West Jersey Seashore Railroad, already servicing Anglesea and Wildwood, extended to the newly opened area. Trains brought fishermen, so many the railroad initiated weekend specials just for anglers. Trains came from Philadelphia via Anglesea. Trolleys conveyed passengers from station to dock where party boats waited to ferry people out to the fishing grounds. The railroad ran a special line to Otten's Harbor on Wildwood's west side to service commercial fleets that ran out of Cold Spring Inlet.

After World War I, Atlantic City Railroad established a siding at Otten's, complete with warehouses, an icehouse and refrigerated cars to handle fish shipments, enabling Wildwood to become the largest fish shipping port on the East Coast south of Gloucester.

Ottens became Wildwood's major harbor, surpassing Anglesea. This happened quickly because Cold Spring Inlet, deepened and fortified with extended rock jetties and given priority maintenance due to the nearby Coast Guard base at Cape May, offered ocean access vastly superior to dangerous Hereford Inlet at the Anglesea end.

When the rum wars escalated, Otten's Harbor played an important role in criminal activities, drawing attention of law enforcement authorities.

Wildwood enjoyed a banner season in 1922. Tourists flocked in to stroll the boardwalk, sunbathe on the beach and splash in the ocean. They came by train and by car.

Aerial view of Otten's Harbor. George F. Boyer Historical Museum.

Prohibition was in effect, but that didn't hamper good times in the least. After all, everybody agreed. "What's the fun at the shore without a drink or two?"

Booze was illegal, but those who wanted it easily got it, while local law enforcement tended to look the other way. The rum fleet kept hotels, cafés and restaurants well stocked with illegal beverage selections. Places like the Elmira, Penn-Wood, Bradley's.

In fact, Rum Row itself became a minor tourist attraction in 1922. According to Harold Waters's book *Smuggling Spirits*, the row entertained daily sightseeing excursions offering out-of-towners a glimpse of real live bootleggers.

Call girls paid the fleet nightly visits. Schooners provided band entertainment and dancing on decks colorfully illuminated by Chinese lanterns. Business was brisk, but there was still time for ship-to-ship carousing.

Authorities were hardly idle. The *Inquirer*, on August 17, described a "flying squadron" of Prohibition agents and state troopers descending on

Wildwood. They conducted door to door searches from Anglesea to Rio Grande Boulevard.

Alarm quickly spread among lawbreakers, while raiders successfully seized $10,000 worth of liquor, loaded it onto a fire truck and shipped it to Atlantic City to store as evidence. Among the establishments raided were "regulars": Windsor Hotel, New Hereford Hotel, Hotel Royal, Hotel Hilton, Inlet House and Biltmore Hotel.

Leaving town through Rio Grande, agents dropped by Tony Carino's Italian grocery store and busted him for six gallon jugs of moonshine and a few cases of beer.

An auspicious Wildwood debut for the area's newest agent: Reverend John B. Adams of Ocean City.

Adams made his first local newspaper appearance in the *Ocean City Sentinel*. On March 16, he arrested Al Williams, charging him with transportation of approximately six quarts of corn whisky found "on his person." Unable to secure bail, Williams was removed to Trenton to appear before the grand jury.

"Bootleggers had better keep shy of Ocean City," the *Sentinel* declared. "Rev. JB Adams, prohibition officer, has a Volstead nose capable of scenting a batch of hooch a thousand miles off."

The paper described Adams as part federal agent, part minister and all "terror to law violators": "His hobby and delight is landing bootleggers in the coop. He takes the shine off moonshine."

His next exploit, the *Sentinel* reported, involved using his detecting skills to nab two likely suspects: "Colored men," the paper noted, who disembarked a local train and were heading into Ocean City.

What gave away their criminal intent? They were carrying suitcases.

Those suitcases required examining, Adams shrewdly deduced. Springing into action, he arrested the pair. Guess what? He was right, netting twelve quarts and a pint for the powers of dry. Adams acquired a nickname, "Fighting Parson," as he expanded his field of operations south into Wildwood.

On his first Wildwood outing, he lived up to his nickname, tussling with bartender Hughie Clark over a pitcher of whisky. The parson won and confiscated the pitcher, contents included. That raid netted fifty cases of beer at Ludy Bishop's place, as well.

Adams returned to Ocean City in late October, participating in a raid that resulted in the arrest of two men for creating a disturbance while under the influence. In this instance, the defendants claimed they'd swapped with a "Polish farmer near Woodbine" a half gallon of paint for a quart of white mule. Considering the mule's kick, they probably would have fared better guzzling the paint.

The pair was fined $12.50 each for disorderly conduct. Adams was dissatisfied with the severity of punishment. He immediately rearrested them for transporting liquor. Adams wanted to know more about that Polish farmer.

Two weeks later, his fortitude paid off. Adams led a raid on the mainland, discovering a "large sized distillery with three stills cooking." Over 250 gallons of whisky, 23 gallons of wine and a quantity of mash were seized. It was Adams's first encounter with home-based liquor industries of the Woodbine area.

But as 1922 drew to a close, lawbreakers in Cape May County felt certain they'd hear more from the raiding parson in 1923.

1923

The Woman's Christian Temperance Union wasn't happy with Prohibition's progress in Cape May County. Meeting in Ocean City in January, WCTU opposed any modifications to the Volstead Act and resolved to "tirelessly" work in upcoming elections to elect candidates dedicated to enforcing the law.

The ladies also held a cake sale.

Lawbreakers weren't buying. In January 1923, men were caught landing illegal booze at Corson's Inlet near Ocean City. The *Sentinel* called it "one of the largest hauls since the dawn of the bootleg era."

Captured goods included four hundred cases of booze, valued at $75,000, one truck, one automobile, one auxiliary cruiser. And fourteen miscreants.

The bust was accomplished by two members of Ocean City's Police Department, George Myers and Edward Seaman. Revolvers drawn, this dynamic duo came upon the smugglers unloading the boat. Encountering resistance, Myers fired, slightly wounding his nearest assailant. That took the fight out of the gang, and all surrendered.

Myers and Seaman allegedly declined a $5,000 bribe to "pretend they hadn't seen anything."

Joining the investigative team in Ocean City was agent John B. Adams. The reverend/cop continued his one-man crusade against Volstead violators. A March 4 *Philadelphia Public Ledger* item described his raid on Max Schwartz's cigar store in Atlantic City. Adams found one hundred pints of whisky along with thirty quarts of assorted liquors. Schwartz protested the liquor was his private stock.

"Tell it to the judge," Adams advised.

Senator Walter Edge ignored Adams's heroics. The Republican announced plans for legislation allowing beer and light wine. With Edge taking a "wet" position, New Jersey's two senators advocated that side of the issue. Democrat Edward Edwards was the other.

Adams ignored Edge as well. The *Philadelphia Inquirer* reported March 9 that the "raiding parson" was also a "fighting" parson. During another raid, Adams encountered bartender Joe Tighe breaking liquor bottles despite orders to desist, while a roomful of the thirsty cheered him on. When Tighe responded to Adams's commands with obscenities, Adams blackjacked him over the head before making the arrest.

The fifty-six-year-old Adams's juices apparently boiled whenever addressed with foul language. Next day, the *New York Times* described Adams tackling a "considerably younger man in court" after that individual employed profanity to denigrate the parson's good work. "Apologize or I'll take you in the street and throttle you to within an inch of your life," Adams demanded.

Adams appeared frustrated with the legal system's handling of Volstead cases he brought to court. He urged sentences of fifteen years' imprisonment for anyone "destroying evidence" in the manner of Tighe. In fact, it was typical for lawbreakers to destroy evidence during raids.

A few days after the *Times* article, Adams was himself arrested, charged with attempted robbery. The complaint was filed by David Feldman, known as "the half-pint king." Adams had raided Feldman's place on four previous occasions. Feldman alleged Adams lacked a search warrant when he seized a quantity of wine. The parson was released on $500 bail.

The *Times*, following the progress of the fighting parson's career, reported that, at his hearing, Adams admitted lacking a warrant but had entered Feldman's store on "suspicion," The magistrate didn't buy it, and Adams was charged with breaking and entering with intent to rob.

The *Ocean City Sentinel* weighed in on its hometown's most famous booze sleuth, noting that the case had aroused considerable interest in legal circles. At issue was whether agents could conduct searches without obtaining warrants, but based upon "observing suspicious activity," a strategy Adams frequently employed.

Did enforcement of the Volstead Act supersede the U.S. Constitution, Feldman's attorney asked, referring to the Fourth Amendment's search and seizure warrant requirement. Even federal Prohibition law required agents to obtain warrants. Unless the agent witnessed violation of the law or "has good reason to believe a violation is being committed in his presence."

Adams's defense was that he perceived lawbreaking occurring everywhere. It was his mission to eliminate it. His superiors argued he always acted within the law and had "established a unique record for stamping out 'blind tigers.'"

Feldman's history didn't help his cause. His priors included busts for maintaining a still and possession of one hundred gallons of moonshine. Undeterred by his legal situation, Adams raided a cobbler's shop where the motto read, "a drink with every half sole, two drinks when rubber heels ordered." Adams, not feeling the least "soleful," seized fourteen quarts of whisky.

***

A new state Prohibition director took over in April, Adrian Chamberlin, Essex County Republican Party chairman. Backed by fellow Republican senator Walter Edge, Chamberlin was appointed after a lengthy political battle that ended with the intercession of President Harding.

Chamberlin's appointment, the *New Brunswick Home News* predicted, would result in "considerable change among the state's Volstead enforcement forces." Field agents faced possibilities of being relieved or relocated.

The raiding parson appeared unconcerned, returning to the pages of the *Times* in late April, loudly denouncing public officials, in an address to local ministers. "Local officials sell whisky and local police do nothing because of pressure from above," Adams thundered. "Whisky comes in by boat. 'Inside' man pays $45 a case. Sells it for $85. Everybody gets a piece of the action."

Adams's simplistic scenario must have enticed bootleggers because the May 19 *Asbury Park Press* reported that the center of "bootleg activity had relocated down coast toward Cape May." The paper added that numerous local businessmen were "in cahoots" with smugglers.

The Coast Guard announced increases in regional manpower, anticipating a "busy summer season." Three bomber planes arrived at Sewall's Point in early May along with two hundred officers and men, ready to fight Rum Row. A dirigible, then under construction at Philadelphia Navy Yard, was slated for assignment to Cape May.

The Coast Guard pledged to establish a cordon to "frustrate" a rum fleet of twelve ships gathered outside the three-mile limit.

The rumrunner *Jerry T* was nabbed off Corson's Inlet near Ocean City by Captain Cornelius Nickerson of the nearby Coast Guard station. Cutters

Hangar at Coast Guard Air Station Cape May. *George F. Boyer Museum.*

patrolled waters off Cape May. In addition to watching for rum smugglers, they were called upon to search for small craft lost at sea during a gale that had recently ripped through the area.

In mid-June, the French arrived. A large French-flagged steamer carrying over twenty thousand cases of choice liquors anchored ten miles off Townsend's Inlet, just above Sea Isle City. Italian fishermen, who had developed a thriving industry at Sea Isle, were watched by authorities, concerned the town's large 'immigrant population" would land the French cargo.

Meanwhile, according to the *Allentown Morning Call*, Adams was "roughly" handled by a woman when he entered a store on a liquor ferreting quest. Fellow officers came to his rescue and subdued his assailant, allowing Adams to secure his liquid prize. The *Sentinel*, Adams's hometown paper, was more sympathetic, describing Adams's assailant as a "virago." The store in question was coincidentally owned by the "half-pint king," Feldman.

This time, Adams had his warrant. Belle Kaufman didn't care. The virago, described as a "robust specimen of femininity, related to Feldman by marriage," operated the store. Unhappy with the parson, she hurled Adams—or "kicked," depending on your witness—across the storeroom until Adams encountered a large plate-glass window.

Crashing through the glass, the man described by the *Sentinel* as "loved as dearly by rum lovers as his satanic majesty loves holy water," landed amid shattered fragments, his dignity intact.

Eventually, several jars of incriminating evidence were secured, and the "tigress" was subdued. The raiders' haul consisted of a coffee pot filled with suspicious liquid and several tumblers containing drink of a "pre-Volstead variety."

Booze and broad were conveyed to jail, where the latter was charged with possession and attempt to destroy the former. No charges were imposed for attempting to destroy the raiding parson.

***

As summer entered the "dog days" of late August, a yacht joined the rum fleet near East End lightship, eighteen miles off Cape May. The yacht was observed hailing a transatlantic liner outbound from Delaware Bay. Forty cases relocated from yacht to liner. Liquid refreshment for the trip across.

While rumrunners busily shifted product, politicians shifted allegiances, solidifying support for Adrian Chamberlin as he settled into his job as the "wettest state's" director of dry.

As matters stood in August 1923, New Jersey's administration of Prohibition was split, with New York's enforcement division assuming charge of cases in northern New Jersey. Reuben Sams, head of Pennsylvania's eastern division, handled cases from Cape May County. Unhappy with the arrangement, Chamberlin headed to Washington, seeking increased manpower so New Jersey agents could enforce the law in New Jersey.

In October, two months into his new assignment, Adrian Chamberlin was on the defensive. He denied allegations that Republican Party officials in counties dominated by that party had exerted pressure on him to "ease up" on illegal booze operators having party connections.

"I don't know," he answered, when asked how much graft was paid since he started. Reporters, as always, loved answers like that. If Chamberlin was looking for solutions to graft and booze problems in New Jersey, he only needed to ask former star agent John Adams.

The raiding parson had returned to the bully pulpit, this time addressing the Clean Government League. Adams offered a resolution to President Coolidge calling for Chamberlin's removal for failing to enforce the dry laws. According to Adams, Chamberlin's "greatest failure" was in furloughing Adams from his agent's job. "Let me go to work and I will enforce the law," Adams declared. "You can't enforce it if senators appoint officers who take orders from local politicians."

The league unanimously adopted Adams's resolution. Members also declared support for a pair of ASL-endorsed candidates for assembly, with the multitalented Adams pegged as campaign manager. Meeting in Sea Isle City, Cape May County's WCTU chapter also called for Adams's reinstatement.

Former U.S. senator Joseph Frelinghuysen and Senator Edge, both Republicans, jousted over the Chamberlin issue for the balance of 1923. Frelinghuysen communicated with Calvin Coolidge, calling for Chamberlin's removal, while Edge rose to his defense.

Democrats sat back and watched the fun. Bootleggers conducted business as usual. The *Trenton Times* provided statistics that supported the beleaguered Chamberlin.

For the period of May 1 through October 20, 1923, Chamberlin-led dry agents conducted 714 raids, confiscating 7,513 cases of beer, 23,365 gallons of liquor, 16,865 gallons of wines, 9,264 kegs of beer and 88 stills. Like diehard baseball fans, dry advocates liked compiling stats. For instance, nationwide from 1920 to 1930, agents arrested 577,000 suspects, with a conviction rate of 66 percent, according to John Kobler's *Ardent Spirit*. Agents seized 1.6 million stills, distilleries and fermenters. They confiscated 9 million gallons of spirits, 1 billion gallons of malt liquor, 1 billion gallons of wine, 45,000 cars and 1,300 boats.

Big numbers.

In the next breath, authorities conceded those figures represented about 5 percent of the total illegal liquor entering the country. The *Times* dismissed anti-Chamberlin rhetoric as political sour grapes from Frelinghuysen, given Chamberlin's connection with political adversary Edge. The paper noted that Chamberlin had been appointed with backing of the ASL and support of then senator Frelinghuysen.

The paper also heaped scorn on certain vocal former Prohibition agents who'd had it in for Chamberlin since he removed them from their posts.

***

When all is confusion and the whole world seems to be in disarray, who will come to the rescue? In 1923, many people thought the answer was the Ku Klux Klan.

On November 29, the *Ocean City Sentinel* reported two burning crosses, one on the Eighth Street beach, the other along the bayside road entering the resort.

No witnesses identified who erected the crosses. The deed was done quickly and quietly, the way the Klan usually did its work.

The paper reported rumors of significant Klan following, with "regular meetings conducted in Ocean City of the 'Invisible Empire.'" Residents

KKK pro–Eighteenth Amendment cartoon. *Cape May Gazette.*

expressed "perfect sympathy" with the Klan's principles and aims, according to the *Sentinel*.

"I hope it's true," one unidentified resident responded when asked if KKK was planning a major move into the resort. "They're needed. There's work for them to do here." The paper estimated about two hundred locals had already enlisted to help the Klan do its "work."

The KKK actually grew in numbers and influence during the 1920s, claiming a peak of 60,000 to 100,000 members in New Jersey by 1925. The Invisible Empire felt sufficiently strong to shed its cloak, pushing issues legislation in New Jersey such as an unsuccessful effort to require the Bible be read to all schoolchildren.

The Klan typically sided with clergymen whose "commonsense 100% American" outlooks on morality welcomed the Klan's support. The Klan's idea of justice was "straightforward, served upon anyone who didn't conform to its idea of Protestant supremacy," according to the *Sentinel*.

Many people were drawn to the Klan because of its stand on Prohibition. Its "program" focused on preventing "heathens" (read: immigrant, Catholic, wet) from destroying the American way of life.

Pro-Klan Methodist ministers, aligned with the Anti-Saloon League, urged congregants to vote Republican, as that party more closely adhered to the Klan viewpoint.

The *Sentinel*'s editorial related to its cross-burning story read like a defense of the Invisible Empire. "Charges [against the Klan] have not been proven because they are fictitious, fabrications of those who have cause to fear the Klan." The editorial writer "refused to believe the Klan was the infamous organization its traducers assert," pointing out that its membership included the "most brilliant minds in the nation."

The Klan stood for "pure and unadulterated Americanism." The paper commended its efforts to enforce the Eighteenth Amendment. "Unfortunately, it's had to veil its actions in secrecy."

Cape May's *Star and Wave* echoed the *Sentinel*'s opinion. Crying out against "poison hooch being sold in grocery stores and fruit stands kept by foreigners," the *Wave* urged the Klan to come to Cape May County, fight Prohibition violators and restore "traditional racial, religious, and social values against foreign threats."

Such was the sentiment of a significant segment of the county population, especially longtime residents. Events staged in support of the Klan drew mainland farmers in numbers to wet Wildwood to attend KKK rallies at Atlantic Pier on the boardwalk.

The *Gazette* reported a local high school rally as "well-attended." Crosses were burned in a Cape May ball park near a "colored neighborhood."

Branches of the Invisible Empire sprouted in Ocean City, Rio Grande and Cape May.

Senator Edge visited Cape May Court House to speak out against the Klan, but crosses continued burning as 1923 drew to a close.

1924

In his book *Black Ships*, Everitt Allen estimated that by 1924, 160 rum vessels operated along U.S. coastal waters. Hundreds of inshore power boats served as couriers from ship to shore, landing more than 100,000 cases of booze a month along the East Coast alone.

The Coast Guard initially fronted an armada of twenty-nine slow-moving cutters to combat this invasion. They captured about the same 5 percent of liquor as their counterparts on land.

But something happened in 1924 to improve the odds weighted so heavily against dry forces: the navy arrived with reinforcements, twenty destroyers and five thousand men.

Entering 1924, liquor sales in Canada soared, with per capita production rising from 9 to 102 gallons per person. Some of the increase was attributed to thirsty Yanks crossing the St. Lawrence for supplies. But most of that liquor flowed seaward to the French-owned island of St. Pierre, which became an important supply terminal supply for Rum Row, rivalling the Bahamas.

To combat this new development, the Coast Guard increased its presence off southern New Jersey, including assuming control of a former World War I naval air station outside of Cape May. The station was located on land formerly owned by Henry Ford who'd planned to build a car plant. Camp Wissahickon was established during the war to drill three thousand navy recruits. The camp was dismantled in 1919.

Once the Coast Guard assumed control, it became that agency's first air station. Eventually, it stationed three amphibious aircraft and seaplanes used both to fight rum and conduct search and rescue missions. The Coast Guard continued to fight a frustrating battle against more appropriately supplied smugglers, whose powerful boats easily maneuvered through shallow water and winding channels to evade the cutters, while their accomplices on land fired upon the pursuit to cover landing operations.

Joseph Burcher describes danger-filled boyhood adventures on the beach in his *Remembering South Cape May*. "We'd sneak out through the second floor window. Shinny down onto the sand dunes and onto the beach," he recalled.

The climbers were drawn by prospects of observing criminals in action. Rumrunners frequently visited South Cape May, a now vanished beachfront village situated between Cape May and Cape May Point. Men drove Chevy trucks at night onto the beach, meeting boats to load kegs and crates full of liquor onto the trucks, Burcher wrote.

The author also recalled CPO Charlie Roseman, a local lad with "family located at Cape May since the 1700's." Roseman captained a patrol boat. "He'd get up close to the beach and fire five inch shells at them [rumrunners]," Burcher wrote. "If they found a crate of beer or whisky they smashed it up."

As the Coast Guard obtained better equipment, the tide gradually shifted in its favor beginning in 1924. Still, some Cape May Countians embraced

South Cape May. *Cape May Point Lighthouse Museum.*

the economic realities of Prohibition, using it as opportunity to develop lucrative "side" businesses.

According to Richard Pierson, in "Reflections on Uncle Dave," David Pierson's Seashore Taxi business really took off in 1924. Before then, he'd provided transportation to and from local churches or Cape May's train station.

Pierson's business increased and changed with the inauguration of "fish train excursions," running as many as twenty cars a day filled with eager anglers, directly from Camden ferry terminal to "head" boat fleets docked at Cape May harbor. By the time the boats returned from a day at the fishing grounds, many of those on board were loaded, typically not with flounder they caught.

Trains back to Camden were frequently missed. Pierson was hired to haul as many as could squeeze into his cab, racing to beat the train to its first stop. Roads in the 1920s were not the best in spite of all the money distributed by county freeholders to beholden contractors. Pierson, playing "catch-up" with his cab, was usually outpaced by the train. So he'd race for the next station. Sometimes, the race ended at Philadelphia.

In the course of playing the game, he developed a network of favorite "stops" along the way. One of Pierson's "regular" stops was Eldora and "Uncle" Sam Sutton's place at East Creek. Refreshment breaks for parched passengers, such stops also allowed the enterprising cabbie to pick up booze to deliver to the city.

Richard Pierson recalled his Cape May home serving as a makeshift warehouse, with "cases of liquor hidden under the bed."

Waiting for the next cab race to Philly…

***

The '20s experienced rapid technology development in communication. In March 1924, the *Wilmington Morning News* described efforts by Secretary of Commerce Herbert Hoover to regulate radio communication to "ensure orderly conduct among users and their multitude of activities requiring oversight."

"Radio communication is not merely a business activity used for private gain," Hoover told Congress. "It is a public concern, same as public utilities." What Hoover didn't tell Congress was that rumrunners loved radio—and not just to listen to Louis Armstrong.

Radio was basically the internet of its time, giving people a common source of information and means of communicating with other people over considerable distance.

Lawbreakers used radio to establish ship-to-shore communication, devising sophisticated code to thwart eavesdropping authorities from learning plans. Well-hidden and guarded radio stations joined the rumrunner arsenal, arranging smugglers' rendezvous and maintaining smooth systems for delivering a steady flow of booze.

***

Reverend John Adams didn't need radio to get out his message. A pulpit would do. Better yet, a newspaper. The parson returned to newsprint on March 10. This time, his target was U.S. Senator Walter Edge.

Addressing a meeting of the Conference of the Central Church, Adams claimed Edge caused him to lose his agent's badge. That single misdeed immeasurably set back Prohibition enforcement in New Jersey, Adams charged. "I can go for a ten-minute walk and get enough liquor to present every minister at this gathering with a case and still have 50 cases left over for myself." Adams flavored his remarks with allegations of corruption at all levels of government.

The following day, the New Jersey Methodist Episcopal Conference passed a resolution demanding Adams's reinstatement. The resolution included an attack on the "moist" leanings of the state's congressional delegation.

The *Philadelphia Inquirer* reported that the Methodist Board of Temperance, Prohibition and Public Morals called upon President Coolidge "to enlist men of the church, if he really intends to enforce the law," guaranteeing a "moisture-proof country within two years."

In other words, let the parson raid!

In two years of service, Adams participated in 350 raids, always armed with two revolvers. Noting that the official reason given for Adams's furlough was "lack of funds," the *Inquirer* offered a solution. "Adams should consider continuing his work merely for the fun he gets out of it."

For once, the parson remained silent.

***

In early April, Cape May County welcomed a new prosecutor to Judge Eldredge's courtroom. Ocean City Democrat William H. Campbell tried two Rio Grande men on possession cases.

"Daren't a man have a quart of whisky for his own personal use?" one defendant asked during proceedings.

"It will pay you to avoid even the semblance of evil," the judge admonished him.

Eldredge decided the new prosecutor was going too easy on the accused in pushing simple possession charges because a still had been found at the scene of the arrest.

"But no makings for liquor," Campbell countered.

Avoiding "evil" or its semblance wasn't in the minds of Ocean City beachcombers that same week. Hundreds swarmed across the sand, hoping to snatch one of the 175 cases of bootleg whisky washing ashore from a distressed rumrunner who'd dumped his merchandise off Ocean City to avoid trouble with authorities.

According to Captain Smith of the local Coast Guard station, empty bottles had been found, while full cases were presumably hidden away by lucky finders. A mini black market opened for selling and buying water-logged merchandise, with prices ranging from $25 to $60 per case.

None of the Ocean City beach sharpies made it to Judge Eldredge's courtroom, but he kept busy with the trial of South Dennis resident Edgar Robinson, arrested for involvement in a rumrunning operation during which four trucks were seized at remote Mosquito Point on Dennis Creek.

Then there was the death of Joseph Smith. The grand jury ruled the twenty-one-year-old Philadelphia man had died from excessive drinking; he had obtained liquor from various county establishments. Indicted were Brighton Hotel, Eugene Springer; College Inn, David McCrossin; Bishop's Hotel, Ludy Bishop; and Busch's Hotel, Anne and Francis Busch. All were charged as "directly responsible" for Smith's death.

More bad news for Volstead violators in Wildwood. The June 6 *Cape May County Times* reported raids on a dozen businesses. Hotels, grocery stores, fruit stands, butchers, bakers—no one was overlooked.

Sheriff George Redding, Police Chief Oakford Cobb, County Detective Umfreed and state police acted in concert making Memorial Day weekend, traditional festive kick-off to summer, a dryer holiday.

Among those arrested were Cosmos and Dominick Cappachione, refreshment stand operators at Otten's Harbor. Officers also nabbed notorious Philadelphia gunman Joe McCann, alias Donnelly. This time he was only packing booze. Making matters worse for thirsty throngs, a sloop carrying three hundred cases of refreshment was blown ashore at Fishing Creek along Delaware Bay.

Law enforcement found the *Etta K* beached, her crew sunbathing nearby. Harry Sawyer, Charles Clegg and Harry Scott were arrested. The liquor was

Copy of complaint authorized by Judge Eldredge. *Dennis Township Museum.*

removed to county jail, as were the sunbathers. The jail was filled to capacity for the long holiday weekend with twenty prisoners and four hundred cases of booze.

Separate cells of course.

Judge Eldredge expressed some "extra"-judicial opinions during the June sentencing of liquor law violators.

Fining Wildwood's Joseph Saks $500 for possession, the judge admonished the father of five. "You ought to be put in a row boat and started back across the ocean to Austria-Hungary from whence you came," he lectured. "Your children are the only ones worthy of consideration from me."

Apparently a trying session for the judge, he also sounded less than magisterial with his comments to Joseph and Mary Mack of Woodbine, accused of possessing material to manufacture liquor. They were caught when firemen, responding to combat a blaze at their house, discovered twenty-five gallons of mash. Mary fought with the firemen, indicating she preferred the house "should burn down." The Macks were repeat offenders, and Eldredge's familiarity with them loosened his tongue. After sentencing Joe to thirty days in jail, he turned to Mary.

"Henpecked by you," he characterized Mary's treatment of Joe.

Ignatz Kischak complaint, signed by assorted authorities. *Dennis Township Museum.*

"I have not the slightest doubt that you're a bootlegger. You've been here before. Here's another from a foreign country come here with the idea she can break the law....If I had my way, I'd put you on the boat alongside Saks."

He sentenced her to sixty days.

Prohibition frayed everybody's nerves, but at least one booze story ended happily this session. The horde taken during Sheriff Redding's raid at Dennis Creek was evaluated by state board of health chemists as "A-1 suitable for medicinal purposes." Instead of being destroyed, the liquor was distributed to three hospitals.

The attention of law enforcement was drawn to mainland areas of the county in the latter part of the year. Especially active were Belleplain, Eldora and Woodbine. Investigating a series of robberies, state police visited a tumbledown shack and found a 25-gallon still, along with 175 gallons of mash. Whisky in progress. Neretta George was arrested, and her husband, Stephen, was nabbed for atrocious assault.

Later that day, Sheriff Redding led a raid on the home of Ignats Klachak. "I make no moonshine," the *Times* quoted Ignats's broken English. A house search turned up nothing. Klachak gave himself away, intently staring at the roof of his barn. Suspicious raiders broke through what turned out to be a false roof, finding the goods.

More raids resulted in the arrest of Michael Kubiak, a farmer near Belleplain who made hay while the moon shined. Redding uncovered a still and quantities of both finished product and working mash in the Kubiak hayloft.

Wildwood wasn't out of enforcement's spotlight for long. The College Inn, a favorite stop for the thirsty and the raiders determined to keep them that way, graduated proprietor David Kirk to the arrested class. Kirk tried destroying evidence, but authorities salvaged plenty of intact bottles to satisfy the judge.

The Brighton Hotel, another regular hit, was ordered padlocked for a year.

Sea Isle City made the Volstead scoreboard with raids at the recently opened Depot Hotel and George Cronecker's Bellevue Hotel.

Meanwhile, county officials raided the farm of John Bogushefsky, four miles outside Woodbine. Apparently, stills had become standard household appliances in that part of the county. No home seemed to be without one. Bogushefsky's was no exception.

Coast guard from Cold Spring and Two Mile stations fired on fleeing smugglers unloading at Fishing Creek, not far from where the *Etta K* had

Chief of Police Oakford M. Cobb (left)
Howard Cattell and Mart Long, May 30, 1923.

Wildwood police chief Oakford Cobb. *George F. Boyer Historical Museum.*

been seized weeks earlier. The bad guys fled into nearby woods, leaving a touring car and 420 five-gallon cans of pure alcohol.

The first half of 1924 ended well for law enforcement, according to the stats. Almost 25,000 gallons of liquor, 4,000 gallons of wine, 622 barrels and 1,015 cases of beer were seized through June, according to the Prohibition Bureau. Agents conducted 1,624 raids, making 846 arrests while confiscating 234 stills.

It wasn't quite so satisfying for Oakford Cobb. Wildwood's police chief was wounded at Two Mile beach by wanted burglar Harry Mason. Mason, who'd been hiding in a cave on the beach, fled the scene after shooting Cobb and exchanging fire with Sargent Lynn Forcum. The August 6 *Inquirer* noted that even though Mason's bullet barely missed Cobb's heart, the "powerful Cobb managed to wrench the gun from his hand."

The chief recovered from his wound and returned to duty. Mason would eventually be shot and killed by his own revolver in a struggle with the police chief of Gloucester City while trying to escape capture in that city.

***

Rear Admiral Frederick Billard declared war on Rum Row. He inaugurated the campaign announcing the reopening of four previously abandoned Coast Guard stations along the Jersey coast. Wildwood station was one

Admiral Billard, USCG. *boatchases.com*.

of the four. Billard did not reveal his "secret plan" for taking on Volstead violators but indicated that twenty recently deployed navy destroyers would participate, with an armada of speed boats assigned to various stations.

The *Cape May County Gazette* reported the reopening of the Wildwood station on August 10, with a full crew under Captain Cornelius Nickerson. The *Gazette* also mentioned over two thousand Coast Guard recruits at Philadelphia Navy Yard preparing to join the "dry navy" for what the paper called "the biggest drive yet to break up rum running along the Atlantic coast."

In addition to destroyers, the navy dispatched sweepers and cabin cruiser patrol boats to hunt back bays and inlets. Enhancing this arsenal was an important change in maritime law. The territorial waters limit was extended out from three to twelve miles.

Ironically, in taking the lead in the rum war, the Coast Guard would return to its original role, conceived by Secretary of the Treasury Alexander Hamilton. In 1790, Hamilton asked Congress for funds to purchase ten cutters to be employed to suppress smuggling. An act of Congress created the Revenue Marine Services.

Manpower issues had long plagued the service. During the Prohibition era, many seamen were foreign born. Perhaps chronically low pay discouraged "natives" from enlisting. Most of these immigrant seamen were, at best, indifferent to the temperance morality underlying Prohibition.

USCG cutter *Seneca*. *www.atlanticarea.uscg*.

"None of us regarded ourselves as crusaders, dedicated to total destruction of Demon Rum," Harold Waters wrote in *Smugglers of Spirits*, his memoir about serving in the Coast Guard. Morale wasn't likely boosted by the quality of vessels on which they served. "Cutter captains and crews, with their old ships that shook to pieces at more than 10 knots, led a miserable existence," Bill McCoy commiserated with his former adversary, recalling hapless cutters going up against much faster shore boats.

That changed in 1924 with the arrival of the new dry fleet. Destroyers made speeds up to eighteen knots. Seventy-five-foot-long patrol boats, armed with heavy machine guns, hit eighteen knots. Both were fast enough to match their quarry.

The law change, extending territorial waters to twelve miles, leveled the playing field as well. Previously, ships flying foreign flags could not be approached outside the three-mile limit unless they had been in contact with shore. Another big change was increased pay for all ranks. Hardly money to match bounties offered by smugglers to servicemen who "played ball" but sufficient to serve as a recruitment incentive.

***

Autumn 1924 witnessed the trial of Louis Bishop, one of the hotel owners indicted following the death of Joseph Smith due to "excessive use of alcohol." Smith had purchased booze at Bishop's Anglesea establishment.

Bishop denied serving Smith, claiming the Philadelphian and his party were "already under the influence" when they appeared at Bishop's hotel. His attorney suggested that Smith's party lied and their word didn't hold as much evidentiary weight as that of a local businessman like Bishop.

Judge Eldredge informed the jury that "sympathy" for the defendant could not be a factor, only the law and whether Bishop had violated it. Bishop was found guilty of serving alcohol to Smith. Trials followed for owners of Busch's Hotel and the Central Inn, with the others to be tried later.

Judge Eldredge had other Volstead cases to adjudicate and wasted little time disposing of Dominick Cappachione. The sixty-three-year-old Wildwood man was sentenced to sixty days in jail, despite insisting he "didn't know about the prohibition law." His attorney blamed Italy in requesting leniency. "Being a native of Italy, he took to liquor like a duck takes to water."

Central Inn, Wildwood. *Dennis Township Museum.*

Prosecutor Campbell noted that this particular Italian duck had given law enforcement problems all summer and his business had been padlocked. New Jersey was no. 1 as 1924 drew to a close.

An Associated Press headline for the day after Christmas declared the state "wettest in the union." Federal authorities celebrated Christmas Eve by capturing a forty-five-foot cabin cruiser, rumored dispatch boat of South Jersey's rum ring. No liquor was found, but on board they found the alleged head of a ring operating thirty-five rumrunners in the area.

The man gave a Maryland Avenue address in Atlantic City. His name? John W. Campbell.

1925

The new year began with the exploding still of Marshall Banks, apparently a very inept moonshiner.

"Since coming to this county from Ohio," Banks whined to Judge Eldredge, "I've been experimenting with sugar, rye, and yeast." Results included two spoiled home brews, an arrest and finally still explosion.

To make matters worse, Marshall's distillery detonation took place within the confines of Ocean City's jail. "I don't know how liquor should be made," Banks explained.

Eldredge sentenced him to sixty days in county jail. Plenty of time for Banks to learn.

***

New Jersey Grange met in Atlantic City, affirmed its support for Prohibition and criticized both of New Jersey's senators. Edge and Edwards introduced legislation to amend the Volstead Act to allow manufacture of 2.75 percent beer.

The Coast Guard had celebrated a much dryer 1924 holiday season, reporting that "only five thousand cases made it" past its cordon. That number compared favorably with the estimated fifty thousand cases that enlivened the 1923 holidays. A mere seven ships composed the rum fleet versus forty in 1923.

Authorities attributed their success to the new speedy thirty-six-foot picket boats used to patrol the outer perimeter of the cordon.

***

The new year also saw resolution of the Bishop case, as Judge Eldredge sentenced the popular Anglesea hotelier to six months in jail plus a $300 fine for serving alcohol to twenty-one-year-old Philadelphian Joseph Smith, who died of "intense alcohol intoxication."

Other proprietors tried after Bishop included Anne and Francis Busch, acquitted. Michael Donnelly, jury dismissed. Eugene Springer and David McCrossin had not yet gone to trial.

This being Bishop's first offense, he remained free on $2,500 bail, pending his appeal to the court of errors and appeals.

***

They were low paid, often uneducated, usually abused by locals who didn't like the Prohibition law. They typically felt no moral imperative to enforce that law. They were tempted with bribes, opportunities to get in on the

Typical Coast Guard crew of the era. *boatchases.com*.

spectacular ill-gotten gains offered by the "other side." All they had to do was nothing.

And yet, a majority of Coast Guardsmen persevered and did their jobs.

Albert Johnson and Albert Hand, surfmen attached to Holly Beach Coast Guard Station, were cleared of any involvement in a rumored bribery scheme instigated by elements seeking to discredit the local station, according to M.W. Rasmussen, Coast Guard superintendent for District 5. The pair was allegedly offered $1,000 (about $15,000 today) to "keep their eyes shut" while cargoes were landed, the *Asbury Park Press* reported.

Johnson described an incident involving the August 1924 seizure near Cape May of the *Ute* carrying twenty-seven cases of liquor. "It was a dark night," he recalled, starting his tale with one of the most familiar lines in detective fiction. "The bootleggers had a car loaded and running."

"What's your price son?" a smuggler asked Johnson, who refused to go along.

"He sped away," Johnson said, "We didn't get him but we got the Ute."

Cornelius Nickerson, Holly Beach station captain, corroborated Johnson's story. He'd concealed himself, overheard the offer and Johnson's

Still with stack of alcohol cans found in woods. *Dennis Township Museum.*

rejection of same. The would-be briber beat a hasty retreat before he could be apprehended.

Meanwhile, there was murder and moonshine in the woods around Woodbine.

Forty-year-old William Camp was shot and killed by twenty-three-year-old woodchopper John Mason at Hoffman's Mill near Belleplain.

The tragedy started as a drinking party at Mason's house. When the liquor ran out, Mason's mother told the partiers, including Camp, that they'd had enough. Camp became physically abusive. He and young Mason had an altercation, and Mason shot him.

Not far from Hoffman's Mill, raiders descended upon the home of Lewis Saduk. They found twenty-five gallons of liquor. Saduk was out on bail for a prior offense, which included a still being found on his property.

Men were caught drinking at Saduk's when raiders appeared. Thomas Brown of Dennisville was arrested for striking a trooper during a brief skirmish between raiders and imbibers. Brown was brought before Jacob Levin, justice of the peace at Woodbine, then sent to county jail. Saduk was fined $200 and sentenced to three months in county jail.

About five hundred bottles were found during this raid. Empties awaiting refill with moonshine bore labels "Pure Rye Whisky. Prepared under the supervision of US government for medicinal purposes." Medicinal liquor was legal under Volstead. The labels indicated this group of lawbreakers was also guilty of false advertising.

"Too bad everybody in this county can't see this," Eldredge said of the label, "to see the way the public is defrauded by vendors of liquor."

Another Woodbine resident was back in court. Joseph Mack was arrested after raiders found two gallons of liquor at his home. Lawbreaking was a family affair at the Mack household in 1925. Missus had enjoyed several get-togethers with the judge. This time, their twelve-year-old son joined dad at court, charged as being "incorrigible."

***

Mislabeled booze, criminal families, incorrigible youth...where would it all end? The WCTU demanded action, issuing an ultimatum that it would fight any sheriff candidate failing to pledge to enforce the dry law. Two men had already tossed their hats in the ring for the Republican nomination: Deputy Sheriff James Hoffman and Wildwood magistrate John Byrne.

The WCTU didn't seem to care as much about gunplay or bank robbery, both of which made local news in 1925.

On March 13, three hold-up men blackjacked Tuckahoe National Bank president Edwin Tomlin, bank cashier Ed Rice and Rice's wife. Tomlin died from his injuries while Mrs. Rice remained an invalid the rest of her life.

The crooks absconded with $700 in a bullet-riddled car shot-gunned by Lilburn Hess, a well-armed neighbor.

Hess managed to wound two robbers. The escape vehicle broke down, and James Pettit, Gus Anderson and Walter Laird were apprehended. The trio were tried on May 14 and found guilty of first-degree murder. Life prison sentences didn't satisfy a public hungry for a hanging.

Frederick Lewis Allen cited a number of reasons for increased violent crime nationwide during the late twenties, including easier access to deadlier weapons, greater mobility with increased automobile use (quicker escapes), growing prominence of gangsters in news media, a wink and a nod attitude to crime attributed to disrespect for Prohibition and a more materialistic society exposed to the greater availability of consumer goods and means of communicating that availability, generating demand.

Perhaps succumbing to pressures exerted by groups like WCTU, beleaguered Prohibition Director Adrian Chamberlin resigned as head of the state's dry force.

***

Michael Donnelly, owner of the Central Inn, previously tried in the "death by alcohol" case of Joseph Smith, was arrested again in late April for liquor law violations.

But the biggest story of the spring of 1925 was the long-anticipated counter attack on Rum Row. The Coast Guard deployed eight picket boats, capable of speeds up to thirty knots and armed with machine guns. They faced off against an international fleet of fourteen vessels, each carrying at least five thousand cases. Located about thirty miles out, the fleet included six steamers (three British, two French, one Belgian) and eight schooners (seven British, one French).

Previous efforts to catch runners at the point of sale had been unsuccessful. Bootleggers implemented a system in which courier craft sped past supply ships, tossing aboard "orders." The order was quickly transferred from the floating warehouse to the courier. This enabled fast-moving couriers to escape before slower law enforcement could position to make arrests.

Smaller, speedier picket boats solved that problem.

Additions to the Coast Guard armada came in three sizes. According to *Smugglers of Spirits*, 100–125 footers, armed with .25-caliber guns and capable of running thirteen knots, were used to shadow supply ships out on the row. The 75-foot craft, also armed and capable of thirteen knots, engaged in open water pursuit of couriers. The 36-footers deployed near shore, guarding inlet entrances, moved fast, up to twenty-five knots, and automobile patrols along beaches covered most likely landing places.

Details of operations were closely kept secrets employing sealed orders, coded messaging and air reconnaissance, conducted on a "war basis." All shore leave was cancelled during operations. In addition, internal "spies"were planted among crews to ferret out suspected cooperation with rumrunners. According to the *Philadelphia Inquirer*, twenty-two boats assigned to coastal waters around Cape May County joined navy destroyers already at sea.

Within a week, Rum Row disintegrated. The Coast Guard successfully cut off all contact with land. After six days, shortages of food and fresh water forced the fleet to disperse. Mother ships either returned to their homelands or moved along to less protected waters.

The blockade's effectiveness was evidenced in one exchange between a rum crewman and Coast Guard seaman as their ships passed close. "We

Schooners anchored at Otten's Harbor. *George F. Boyer Historical Museum.*

need water," the former shouted. "How about 100 cases of whisky for 100 gallons of water?"

While this effort succeeded, it by no means ended the war. Coast guard officials acknowledged that "enormous caches of booze" had already been landed, safely hidden away for future sales. One of those hiding places was at Consolidated Fisheries plant near Wildwood, where as many as one thousand cases at a time were landed by fishing boats doing double duty.

Consolidated offered a number of advantages to rumrunners. It was close to the busy fishing port of Otten's Harbor. It offered access to Cold Spring and Turtle Gut (before it was filled) and Hereford Inlets. Consolidated provided a refrigerated warehouse and access to rail transportation. A ring of speakeasies and "juice joints" circled the harbor, giving booze purveyors a quick and easy way to unload merchandise. Not to mention that Consolidated was owned by the Hiltons, not especially sympathetic to the dry cause.

Wildwood remained drenched despite efforts to dry up Cape May County. Violators ran the gamut from rumrunner to rum consumer. Local businessmen made no secret of their antipathy toward Prohibition, seeing it as inimical to their interests, which relied heavily upon catering to every

Barrels of fish being loaded at Otten's Harbor ice plant. *George F. Boyer Historical Museum.*

whim of seasonal tourists. Summer resorts needed to "breathe freedom of soul and body," an unidentified man of commerce complained to the *Five Mile Times*.

Operators of so-called "juice joints" cleverly concealed their activities. They created passwords, fake front operations and membership cards. They designed physical changes to their buildings, placing stills behind walls, fitted with rubber hoses connected to kitchen sink fixtures to dispense whisky, gin—booze selection depended on whether you picked "hot" or "cold."

Many of these establishments were also brothels, such as Chester Dick's Harbor Inn. The feds puzzled for years over where the place hid its booze. Years later, while the building was being razed for more modern construction, two tanks were discovered inside the wall.

Boats, including elements of the local fishing fleet, handled so much booze that the stench rising from the harbor often reeked more of whisky than mackerel as operators dumped "evidence" into the harbor whenever a raid was expected.

Local law enforcement was often reluctant to interfere with illegal business. On one occasion, a Wildwood officer allegedly interfered with a federal raid at the notorious Hotel Bradley. In July, officer Michael Sheehan was beaten by federal agents when he interfered with a raid in progress. In return, Wildwood cops obtained warrants to arrest the feds, led by Willard Barcus.

Depending on whose version of facts you believe, raiders showed their warrant to the Bradley's bartender, who tried destroying two pitchers filled with evidence. The agent intervened and poured the liquid into an evidence bottle. Sheehan interfered with the agent. A tussle ensued.

Sheehan was subdued after an agent allegedly conked him over the head with a bottle—not the precious evidence bottle. Sheehan was taken to Mace Hospital to be sewed up.

Meanwhile, Wildwood PD arrested the feds. The feds promised counter charges.

After securing the Bradley evidence, the undeterred Barcus led his agents on raids at McCardell's Inn at Holly Beach and Inlet House at Anglesea. Booze was found at both locations.

Sheehan drew a thirty-day suspension for his part in the ruckus. His defense, that he thought the agents were shaking down the Bradley, didn't hold water—or any other liquid.

Otten's Harbor played a significant role, not just during Prohibition, but as a fishing port throughout the early history of Wildwood. The island's involvement in local fishing traced back to the whaling days of the seventeenth century, and its first tentative inhabitants were fishermen who built seasonal shacks at the north end of the island.

In the early twentieth century, the Anglesea Association took a census of its fishing fleet and counted 486 working boats of various sizes. After much of the industry shifted to Otten's Harbor, the railroad followed. Regularly scheduled trains brought day-trippers to the party boats and carried away the commercial catch to markets like Atlantic City and Philadelphia, as much as one million pounds a year.

When Henry Otten came to Wildwood, he was not interested in fishing. He was a real estate man, with a keen eye toward the future of Five Mile Beach. He was joined in his vision enthusiastically by fellow entrepreneur and sometimes partner, Augustus Hilton.

Otten opened his first real estate office at Anglesea, already a bustling community based around the lighthouse and featuring thriving fishing docks along with hotels and cafés to serve those coming to wet their lines. He built the largest hotel on the island and donated land for a city hall and a fresh-air home for needy children. Otten also published the *Leader* newspaper.

And every year at Christmas, he played Santa Claus for local youngsters. Every kid got shoes, clothing, coal, food—whatever they needed.

Originally active in the north end of the island, Otten looked south, developing the harbor that today bears his name. Closer to the well-maintained Cold Spring Inlet, Otten's Harbor emerged as the area's primary port. Warehouses, icehouses and related businesses rapidly sprang up in the surrounding area.

Among these was the Consolidated Fish Company.

***

A few days after the feds' eventful Wildwood adventure, state police and county detectives raided a bakery at Arctic Avenue near Otten's Harbor.

They found the goods, distilled, not baked. A pitcher and a teapot both filled with illegal brew. Raiders moved south to Cape May, returning to the Tangerine Café where they found three bottles of "coloring" used to "authenticate" adulterated booze and bottles of "finished" product. Colorings were used to disguise alcohol, allowing sellers to pass it off as higher quality brands, a common practice among lawbreakers.

Whisky, in its original state, is clear. In England, it was aged in sherry barrels, giving it a yellowish-gold tint. American distillers aged it in burned barrels. After several years, the charred wood of the barrel turned the whisky a rich amber shade. To simulate those colors, bootleggers employed assorted coloring substances, including creosote. They enjoyed limited success in matching the originals, but desperate drinkers seldom objected.

**

Liquor war raged into the fall on both land and sea—and even underground.

On October 17, the *Wildwood Tribune Journal* described a raid by county and state forces on the "small hamlet outside Woodbine called the Ludlam Tract, inhabited solely by Bohemians." Officials arrested Frank Skipalo. Again. Skipalo had been arrested previously, but charges were dropped due to lack of evidence.

Not this time.

County Detective Umfreed led his squad into the woods, toward Eldora. At one point, Umfreed stepped into what he thought was a rabbit hole. The ground gave, revealing an opening. A ladder descended into the underworld.

The cops entered a 250-square-foot chamber, finding a fully vented forty-gallon still, kerosene stove, cold water system and numerous fifty-gallon barrels of mash. Frank Skipalo's still.

Raiders weren't finished with Woodbine. They returned to Ignatz Kisback's place, busting him again, his third offense. The haul included a fifteen-gallon still and unspecified quantity of mash.

Raiders returned to the islands. The Tangerine Café in Cape May was revisited and proprietor Samuel Rosenberg arrested, also for the third time. Sam tried destroying evidence, two bottles of whisky, but agents were too quick for him.

Prosecutor Campbell, presenting this case to the jury, employed an unusual strategy, indicating he personally opposed the law he was prosecuting. "The jury may not be in sympathy with the Hobart [New Jersey's modified Van Ness liquor] law. I'm not in sympathy with it," he explained. "But the sovereignty of the state is at issue. It's your duty and mine to uphold the laws the legislature sees fit to enact."

The strategy worked. The jury deliberated under ten minutes before returning a guilty verdict.

Familiar names appeared in local papers under what could have become a regular feature: "The Padlocked Report." October's entries from Wildwood included Bradley Hotel, Hotel Royal, Elmira Hotel and Inlet Hotel (Anglesea).

1926

Another new year. Another raid in Wildwood. This year, it was Sheriff James Hoffman's turn to lead. Hoffman swooped down upon the Pacific Hotel, finding a large quantity of liquor and a proprietor to arrest, Jonathan James.

Raiders discovered a secret trap door leading to a compartment beneath the floor of the saloon. There, they found nine cases of scotch, five gallon cans of alcohol, five gallon demijohns of whisky and eighteen bottles of assorted liqueurs.

The James case evolved along a more interesting line than typical possession cases. His attorney petitioned the court to enjoin the prosecutor from using the seized alcohol as evidence against his client. What's more, because of "flaws in the warrant," he demanded the liquor be returned to James. The "flaw" was the warrant's failure to specifically list the property and location to be searched.

Unlike many of his peers, James did not deny owning the hotel or the seized liquor. The court ultimately ruled in James's favor, ordering Hoffman to return the booze. But, the *Wildwood Tribune Journal* reported, James never reached home with his recovered property. Returning from Cape May Court House in triumph, liquor in hand, James was stopped by Hoffman near Wildwood Golf course. He was again arrested and his cargo seized.

This time, the charge was transporting illegal liquor. This new sheriff was either a sore loser or a man to be reckoned with.

Hotel Pacific, Wildwood. *George F. Boyer Historical Museum.*

***

The new year marked the beginning of the end of the railroad's dominance as the means of reaching Cape May County. Construction of the Ben Franklin Bridge linking Philadelphia to Camden across the Delaware River completed, travelers abandoned trains with their inconvenient schedules in favor of freedom of the road offered by the automobile as they crossed rural areas of the county to reach seaside resorts of their choice.

Local roads weren't paved in some rural areas. And there were no superhighways: no Atlantic City Expressway, Garden State Parkway or Route 55.

Some tourists still took the train, and starting early in the twentieth century, each of the islands offered connecting service to the outside world.

It didn't matter how some people traveled—sooner or later, they arrived in Judge Eldredge's courtroom. That was the case with Charles Bradley. In the first court session of 1926, Eldredge fined Bradley $500 for possession and added a not-too-subtle warning. "I could send you to county jail for this [infraction]," he told Bradley. "Next offense means state prison."

Hugh McCardell of McCardell's Inn was also fined $500 for having 124 pints of alcohol on premises, found during a pre-Christmas raid. McCardell got the message. He tore out the inn's bar and began the process of selling his property, a not uncommon reaction from convicted Volstead offenders among Wildwood's business community.

The case of Robert Moore, owner of the Inlet Hotel in Anglesea, was postponed due to lack of court stenographer, but Moore saved time and taxpayer expense of a trial by pleading guilty. He was fined $400, and the Inlet House was padlocked. Moore subsequently sold the property.

It was commonly known that speakeasies in the Hereford Inlet area openly flouted the law, especially during the off season. George Boyer's *Wildwood, A History* mentioned that Moore's enjoyed frequent deliveries from England and Russia, "practically delivered to the door."

During Prohibition, crews of clam boats docking at the inlet often stayed at Inlet House. Mother ships loaded with cases of European liquor anchored outside Hereford Inlet. Smaller courier boats, attempting to land their booze, raced pursuing Coast Guard. When the pursuit closed in, the smugglers allegedly tossed their cargoes onto a nearby sand bar. Some locals insist this is how today's Champagne Island, between North Wildwood and Stone Harbor, acquired its nickname.

Next trial was Nicholas Turchi, alleged operator of a speakeasy near Otten's Harbor. A native of Italy, Turchi wasn't sure how to plead to the possession charge. "It's up to you," he told Eldredge.

Turchi acknowledged formerly owning a Philadelphia saloon. He told the court that raiders had confiscated "leftover supplies" from that business that he'd brought to Wildwood. For "personal use."

"None of it was sold," he told the court. Turchi's case was postponed.

Another case that had been dragging along drew closer to resolution when indictments were returned against David McCrossin, Michael Donnelly and Eugene Springer, hotel proprietors accused of selling liquor to Philadelphian Joseph Smith, who died during what the *Gazette* called "a drinking orgy" a year earlier.

Finally, there was Scotty, the defendant who served as his own lawyer. And won. W. Scott Errickson was tried for possession and pleaded not guilty. He cross-examined several government witnesses who conceded his place on the bayside at Pierce's Point was a restaurant and headquarters for fishing parties.

Detective Umfreed testified that raiders had found several boxes marked "white mule."

"I rent buildings and hire out boats," Errickson said in his own defense, claiming to be unaware of his customers' belongings. The liquor had been found in buildings he'd rented to the Fishing Club of Philadelphia, he said. He also denied being present during the raid, nor was he issued a search warrant by the raiding party.

Based on the evidence and Scotty's performance, the jury found him not guilty. Detective Umfreed wasn't discouraged by the Errickson verdict. He continued leading raids through the balance of January. He destroyed stills in Woodbine, found liquor under counters in Cape May stores and destroyed those 124 pint bottles of booze obtained during the McCardell raid.

***

The *Philadelphia Public Ledger* March 4 edition reported New Jersey governor A. Harry Moore's "vigorous campaign against activities in low criminal resorts and roadhouses." Democrat Moore roundly criticized county prosecutors for their "lax attitudes in prosecuting certain types of cases."

"What constitutes a roadhouse?" The *Gazette* demanded clarification of the apparently new term, possibly a by-product of America's new fascination with automobile travel. The paper answered its own question. Roadhouses were described as "public places where alcoholic liquor is sold without even the semblance of secrecy and where five to fifty cars are parked on summer nights 'til long past bed time." Readers might easily surmise the *Gazette* editor had one or two specific establishments in mind when he wrote that.

While folks on land debated the particulars of roadhouses, at sea the Coast Guard scored a major victory against a much-weakened Rum Row. The cutter *Seneca* captured the 235-foot "pirate" ship *Donetta*, flying a U.S. flag near the Delaware Capes in early March. The *Donetta*'s entire thirty-man crew was drunk when boarded. No one was in charge. Pretty good description of your typical "pirate" ship—only this one carried illegal gold of a liquid variety: $1.42 million in booze.

According to the Coast Guard, *Donetta* had been sailing out of control since leaving Florida. The boarding party found crewmen swilling champagne from buckets or guzzling directly from bottles. All aboard were "obstreperous, boisterous, and roaring drunk." All that was lacking was a one-legged man, talking parrot perched on his shoulder.

The prize was towed to New York, where an inventory counted 500 drums of Belgian alcohol, 90 gallons each; 7,000 cases of champagne, valued at

$125 per case; 7,500 cases of Italian wine; Scotch whisky; and other high-octane liquors.

The absence of licensed officers and registration documentation on board allowed the Coast Guard to officially designate *Donetta* a "pirate ship." Like anyone had any doubts.

***

Judge Eldredge returned to the bench in March, imposing sentences in three previously adjudicated Wildwood liquor cases. Patrick Bradley, owner of Club Café, was fined $400 after pleading guilty to possession after insisting the liquor seized was for his personal use. Rocco Lobato also pleaded guilty to possession. The grocer paid a $300 fine for a quart and a pint of booze. J.P. Rakestraw, arrested during a raid on the Central Inn, had denied being an employee of the establishment, though conceded he was "in charge of the place" when raiders hit. Two bottles were found on his person. He was fined $125 per bottle.

The *Cape May Gazette* wondered if those cases would be the last heard by Judge Eldredge. His future on the bench hung in political limbo, held up by

Henry Eldredge House in West Cape May. *Cape May Historical Society*.

political power plays in Trenton. Henry Eldredge was originally endorsed by the Cape May County Democratic Party to complete the term of the late Curtis Baker in 1913. That stint was followed by his own five-year term, reappointed by Governor James Fielder.

Born in West Cape May in 1881 to "Mayflower" parents (Henry Eldredge married Emma Reeves, and both families were original county settlers before the American Revolution), Eldredge was educated in Philadelphia, earning science and law degrees at the University of Pennsylvania in 1907.

Upon returning to the county, he worked as cashier at Merchant National Bank of Cape May. He would one day be named president of that bank. He became an attorney in 1910. At age thirty-two, he was appointed to fill Baker's seat on the bench of the Court of Common Pleas. A Democrat in a Republican-dominated county, Eldredge never let politics affect his behavior on the bench.

Prohibition changed the nature of his work dramatically, with a preponderance of his cases being liquor-related.

Eldredge was a teetotaler in his personal life. He didn't allow that preference to bias his judgment. However, he believed it his duty to uphold the law because it was the law. He tended to show leniency to first-time offenders.

His perspective can best be summed up in his own words, a jury address: "Your own perceptions about Prohibition should have nothing to do with your verdict. There is a law against selling liquor. As long as there exists such a law, it must be enforced."

Of course, not all his cases were boozy.

On one occasion, he shared child rearing advice in the case of twelve-year-old Walter Hines Jr. of Wildwood, accused of being "incorrigible": "For trouble with children, there's no substitute for a shingle in the wood shed."

That same session, Eldredge expressed his view about wrongdoing near the other end of the life cycle. The case involved seventy-three-year-old Helen and seventy-five-year-old John Applebee of Dennisville. The couple pleaded "no contest" on charges of possession and maintaining a disorderly house. Helen watered the courtroom floor with tears as her attorney pleaded for mercy. Eldredge suspended the couple's sentence but not without having his say.

"You and your husband should be getting ready for the next world," he admonished.

According to Michael Conley, whose article on the judge appeared in *Cape May County Historical Society Magazine*, he was "well liked and respected for his fairness and honesty. The consensus was that he 'couldn't be bought.'"

His supporters argued that this very fact was why detractors wanted him off the bench. In 1926, Eldredge's reappointment was held up in Trenton by a maneuver known as "senatorial courtesy," initiated by State Senator William H. Bright, a Wildwood Republican. Critics of Bright's accused him of working on behalf of bootleggers, but there was no evidence of anything much more than political gamesmanship.

In a March 19 editorial, the *Gazette* summed up the situation, stating that Eldredge's twelve-year tenure had been "unimpeachable": "But he is not a

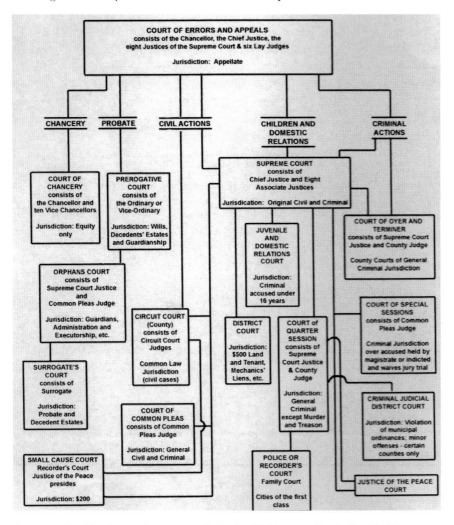

Chart showing New Jersey's legal system during Prohibition era. *Dennis Township Museum.*

politician. He labors under the impression that courts and politics should be divorced and justice administered in the manner pleasing to the citizen but not necessarily to the politician."

Governor Harry Moore, who'd submitted Eldredge for approval, had a more direct take on the situation. "Law abiding citizens of Cape May County will not permit the opposition of bootleggers to prevent the appointment of Judge Eldredge." The grand jury formally protested the lack of a judge, "a deplorable and inexcusable condition in the county court."

The situation affected the workings of the entire local legal apparatus. The grand jury handed down indictments, but with no judicial authority to implement them, action was delayed.

Bright and Moore remained entrenched in their respective positions as the state legislature recessed. The attorney general added to the dilemma by ruling that Moore could not unilaterally reappoint Eldredge, freezing any decision until the legislature returned.

Mike Sheehan, Earl Maxwell, Harry Tenenbaum. *George F. Boyer Historical Museum.*

Bright, the *Gazette* reported, had no comment. Bright wanted Moore to name fellow Wildwoodian Samuel Lanning to the county tax board. Moore opposed Lanning because Lanning was identified with the KKK, which had opposed Moore's election as governor.

With stalemate in Trenton, there would be no action for at least two months until the legislature reconvened. For stopgap, Cumberland County judge Herbert Bartlett heard cases in Cape May County part-time.

Bright's nine-year Senate career ended with the next election. His role in the Eldredge controversy contributed to his defeat. Eldredge's career on the bench would resume and flourish.

***

While politicians dithered over the judge's fate, the Coast Guard fought internal legal battles.

The April 23 *Gazette* reported proceedings involving bribery charges against six petty officers. All were boatswains commanding rum chaser operations out of Cape May. The men allegedly took bribes totaling $10,000, in connection with a major liquor seizure, valued at $250,000, in late 1925.

Cronecker's Hotel, SIC. *Sea Isle City Historical Museum.*

The man who supposedly offered the bribes was Earl Maxwell, a Wildwood man allegedly invested in the illegal enterprise. The money was paid for "protection" in landing the liquor. Maxwell turned witness against the boatswains when he demanded and they refused to repay the bribes after the operation failed and the booze was seized.

Five of the accused were found guilty and sentenced to terms of up to one year in the naval prison at Portsmouth, New Hampshire. The *Wildwood Journal Tribune* noted that the sixth man, Henry Manning, had "witnessed" but did not participate in the scheme.

***

With busy summer approaching along with the arrival of a new state Prohibition director, F.T. Baird, raids increased around Otten's Harbor and more air power was applied against smugglers.

Five planes stationed at Cape May Naval Air base provided constant aerial surveillance over southern New Jersey waters. The mainland war also escalated with raids around Woodbine netting arrests and materials.

"Temporary" Judge Bartlett tried Mrs. Nicholas Ciabatoni, operator of a store above her husband's garage in Woodbine. Found guilty of selling liquor, she was "shown mercy" as a first-time offender. Raiders employed a different tactic to capture the lady bootlegger, sending in a minor prior to raiding to purchase whisky.

Agents also struck Sea Isle City. Owner of Cronecker's Café George Cronecker, former Sea Isle mayor, was sentenced to one week in county jail.

More danger-filled was the raid on Rosario Criurelli's place, where a state trooper was attacked by a hammer-wielding proprietor after raiders found a two-gallon jug of liquor. Rosario first offered agents a roll of bills, about $200. When that was declined, he tried some smashing—first the jug, then the trooper's skull.

It wouldn't be a raiding spree without visiting a favorite haunt in Wildwood, the Elmira Hotel, where Richard Bradley was arrested. Proving the old adage that it's all about location, Bradley claimed he was actually a real estate salesman and had only gone behind the bar to fix a broken cash register. Richard Curran, alleged proprietor, backed his story. Both were arrested, and Elmira was padlocked. The hotel was another Wildwood establishment known to thirsty tourists and locals—and the feds. Elmira openly flaunted the law, advertising the sale of high-powered beer in plain sight.

Rum Row was in decline, but booze still seemed to be everywhere in Cape May County, even aboard the cement ship. Today, it's a tourist attraction at Sunset Beach on Delaware Bay near Cape May Point. Tourists drive to the bay front and browse the gift shop for Cape May diamonds.

It sits just off the beach, protruding from the water. The decaying remains of a concrete ship, the *Atlantus*.

Actually, the hull.

The *Atlantus* was transported from Maryland, intended to serve as a dock for a ferry that would run from Cape May to Lewes, Delaware. Upon arrival, *Atlantus* sank in shallow water. Plans for the ferry were changed.

Even as the monolith was moved into position, rumors circulated that its owner had stowed aboard 1,500 cases of whisky. Coast Guard patrols were dispatched to investigate, and the ship was boarded and searched. No booze.

"That hull," the absolved owner self-righteously declared, "is absolutely dry. It doesn't even hold water."

***

Raiders kept working to assure a dry summer in 1926. They visited the Hotel Brighton in Wildwood twice, witnessed a car accident at Ocean City and seized three pints of booze from one of the drivers before returning to Wildwood, raiding the Penn-Wood Hotel and following that with a repeat engagement at the Pacific Hotel, where they arrested five, including owner Jonathan James.

Not to be outdone by the feds, a combined contingent of state, county and local law enforcement hit Café Henri in Cape May, arresting owner Henri Borbach. Borbach also owned Club Madrid in Philadelphia. Two gallons of martini fixings (gin and vermouth) were confiscated.

Following an anonymous tip, lawmen hastened to Otten's Harbor and, for the third time, visited the establishment of Rocco Turchi. Previous raids had uncovered nothing, but this time, sleuths found tanks embedded in the upstairs walls. Coils ran down to the ground floor, where they connected to faucets in the kitchen sink. Plumbing, Wildwood style. The entire apparatus, dismantled, was taken in evidence along with twenty gallons of liquor.

The cops headed for the Dew Drop Inn (formerly Holly Beach Yacht Club). They found more liquor hidden in the walls but no elaborate setup like Turchi's. One of those arrested was a "colored man who did business at Stone Harbor." He was given a choice, "leave town or go to jail."

This unusual sentence might have been initiated by a petition, signed by numerous members of the local black community, urging authorities to do something about this individual. His sentence and $100 fine suspended, the man left Cape May County to return to his native North Carolina.

Judge Bartlett's resolution of that case probably didn't sit well with the WCTU. At its annual convention held at Wildwood's First Baptist Church, the organization demanded "mandatory jail time" for Volstead violators in addition to or instead of monetary fines. Members were even more frustrated with the ongoing "death by alcohol" case initiated in 1924.

Arrested, convicted and sentenced to six months in county jail, Ludy Bishop remained a free man while his case worked through the appeal process. Finally, in late autumn, Bishop accepted his fate, surrendering himself to the sheriff to begin his sentence. While Bishop turned himself in, his many friends circulated a petition seeking his early release. About a thousand signatures were obtained.

When the court of errors and appeals finally affirmed his conviction, Bishop appealed for "relief." Judge Harry Burt Ware granted a stay and listened to still more testimony. Ultimately, he too affirmed the decision.

Six months for Ludy. Bishop resigned himself to doing time. But suddenly, Bishop was freed.

After Bishop served a week, Judge Ware released him on December 23. Ware wrist-slapped him on the wallet, fining him $300. Why Ware's sudden change of heart?

Holiday spirit? Perhaps some other kind?

***

All was calm for Christmas on Rum Row now that the Coast Guard had matters well in hand. "Our patrols between Atlantic City south to Five Mile Light report one rumrunner cruising," authorities at Cape May announced. That cruiser was far east of Cape May, out of touch two hundred miles at sea.

The Coast Guard's "air force" made sure that 1926 in Cape May ended on a dry note. But that didn't mean the year's end would be dull. This time, the courtroom itself provided the drama.

The Drummond case, reported by the *Gazette*, introduced readers to the Guarantee Detective Agency, a private investigator out of Atlantic City. George Drummond of North Wildwood was arrested for selling liquor out of his home to operatives from the agency, working for the county prosecutor.

Drummond's defense opened with unsuccessful arguments about deficiencies with the warrant and vagueness of the indictment. But the heart of the defense case was the character and veracity of the prosecution witnesses, namely, operatives of Guarantee Detective Agency.

The facts of the case seemed straightforward enough. In June, the defendant sold two pints of whisky to John Delany, a.k.a. Rae, Edward Potts, a.k.a. Batt, and Ralph Crooks of many aliases. All worked for Guarantee. Drummond was paid four dollars for the 48 percent alcohol.

Perhaps all those aliases should have suggested that all might not be what it seemed.

Guarantee had been hired by the county prosecutor's office to assist with liquor-related investigations, but the agency became entangled in a dispute with the county over bills submitted for guarding booze stored at the county jail, further casting shadow on Guarantee's operations. Delany didn't make a convincing witness. He admitted he didn't know where he'd been before going to Drummond's house. He was fuzzy about where he went afterward.

Potts was equally unclear.

Drummond swore that Potts had never been to his home, only Delany and Crooks. And it was with Crooks that he'd dealt. The *Gazette* noted that Crooks, at the time of Drummond's trial, was himself under arrest for attempted extortion. Drummond conceded he supplied booze for Crooks but "made no profit from it."

Another witness testified that Delany got very drunk at his place, waving a revolver and badge while demanding more liquor, which he drank for two hours.

The jury, clearly unhappy with the quality of Guarantee's employees, ruled for Drummond. That was just the opening act for the men (and women) of Guarantee Detective Agency.

The next case involved Margaret Stanton, proprietor of the Hilton Café, on trial for possession. But it appeared more that Prosecutor William Campbell and his private detectives were being tried, as defense attorney John Wescott, a former judge, described the sleuths as "rats" and "questionable trash." He castigated Campbell for hiring them.

"It's a money making job," Wescott charged. "The young prosecutor's political ambitions motivated him to hire these outside detectives to increase his conviction rate." Campbell countered that the former judge's theatrics were an attempt to divert attention from facts of the case, again apparently straightforward.

On June 10, operative John Delany purchased two glasses of whisky at fifty cents apiece, at Hilton Café. He drank booze at the café on four separate occasions. His undercover drinking paid him five dollars per day plus expenses. He was accompanied by a young-looking woman identified as his wife. She drank as well.

The defense countered with character witnesses, including North Wildwood mayor George Redding. A maid at the café testified the business sold only near beer. Stanton told the court she'd been approached by Ralph Crooks, Delany's "partner." Crooks tried extorting $500 for protection. Insinuating that the whole affair was a setup, she said when she turned down Crooks, the Delanys appeared.

Wescott then called a "surprise" witness. County Prosecutor William H. Campbell.

Their interaction didn't touch upon any of the particulars of the Stanton case. Instead, Wescott challenged Campbell's motives for hiring an outside agency over using county detectives. Campbell said he expected the increase in arrests would offset the cost of hiring Guarantee.

Wescott also accused the prosecutor of singling out Wildwood for heavy raiding while ignoring Ocean City, home to the Campbell family. His father, William Sr., served on the Ocean City Council. Campbell denied the allegation.

The jury deliberated several hours but failed to reach a verdict. Ten favored acquittal. The jury was discharged.

But that wasn't the end of the Guarantee Detective saga.

One member of that cast, Ralph Crooks, was first arrested by County Detective Umfreed in Wildwood during the summer, on a complaint from local hotel men that Crooks attempted to extract "hush" money. Crooks was released on $200 bail. A few weeks later, Crooks was again arrested—this time in Ocean City, on a warrant sworn out by his former employer, Guarantee Detective Agency.

The agency contended Crooks possessed evidence needed in its dispute with county freeholders over payment of a $2,000 bill it had submitted for services rendered.

The forgotten man in this year's closing melodrama, County Detective Charles Umfreed, had the last word, as reported in the *Gazette*. "Resigned."

Having worked for the prosecutor's office for several years, Umfreed blamed his boss for his decision to leave. Campbell had indicated to Umfreed that the freeholders pressured him into cutting expenses in his department. Campbell reduced Umfreed to part-time employment earlier in 1926, as part of that economizing. Umfreed learned that money had never been an issue. Campbell wanted more cash to pay for his private detectives.

The year ended, promising that 1927 would bring more headaches for the county prosecutor.

1927

In 1927, Prohibition proponents lost their most powerful voice when Anti-Saloon League's Wayne Wheeler died. To many, Wheeler was the ASL. He is credited with creating the single-issue lobby. During this era, he was arguably the most powerful unelected man in American government, such was his ability to make or break political careers.

Unsympathetic to those he called "morally corrupt" for insisting on drinking, Wheeler was uncompromising in his opposition to alcohol, successfully pushing for insertion into the law a clause requiring the addition of toxic methanol to alcohol legally produced for industrial uses.

Edward Edwards accused him of murder for his advocacy. Wheeler never flinched. "The person who drinks it [industrial alcohol], is a deliberate suicide." Wheeler declared.

In 1927, the year-round population of Cape May County was 29,486 higher by 10,000 than 1920. Barrier island resorts Ocean City, North Wildwood and Wildwood showed the greatest growth. Seasonal population exceeded 400,000.

In 1927, the county had 102 miles of paved road. That same year, Alfred Cooper relinquished his editorship of the *Cape May County Gazette* after forty-eight years. When he started the paper, published on the corner of Main and Mechanic Streets in Cape May Court House, resort towns on the county's barrier islands were mostly barren sand bars.

In 1927, Anheuser Busch introduced Bud Yeast, which the company sold along with its near beer, Bevo. The company also sold a line of products

Alfred Cooper, *Gazette* publisher. *Dennis Township Museum.*

for home brewers, including malt syrup. "We ended up being the biggest bootlegger supply business in the country," August Busch Jr. joked after Prohibition was repealed.

In 1927, Cape May County jail expanded to house eighty prisoners, including eight females. The reason? Overcrowding due to the number of convicted liquor law violators. The cost of feeding prisoners was 48.5 cents per day.

In 1927, Prohibition reached the halfway point in its history. The war against Rum Row was largely over, but individual bootleggers and organized smuggling syndicates still caused headaches for law enforcement. The battle intensified in courtrooms as violators devised new strategies to avoid incarceration. Forces of the law often turned on one another frustrated at being unable to eliminate booze once and for all.

The year 1927 began with former judge Wescott again facing off against County Prosecutor Campbell. Guarantee Detective Agency was again the subject, but Wescott represented a new client: Campbell's bosses, the Cape May County Freeholders.

Wescott lambasted the detective agency for its "improper accounting methods" during a suit filed by Marcus Carroll, the agency's owner, seeking to recover $2,694 for Guarantee's work during the previous summer. The freeholders refused to pay Carroll's bill. Wescott asserted that Carroll's operatives essentially ran an extortion racket in Wildwood.

Campbell, who'd hired the agency, originally authorized payment. His decision had been certified by Judge Bartlett. A higher court affirmed Bartlett's ruling, adding a caveat stating the county could avoid paying if it could show fraud by Guarantee.

Enter former judge Wescott.

"Every one of these agents was himself a criminal," he claimed, contending they were more interested in extorting money than performing the "slight service" they provided, which, he insisted, could have been provided by detectives already on county payroll.

Wescott accused the prosecutor of exceeding his authority in hiring the agency. In office since 1924, Campbell argued that state law empowered him to do what he did and that he'd discussed the matter with Judge Bartlett, with the judge approving the idea. Campbell also defended the agents, saying they'd "employed reasonable diligence" in their work.

Wescott barraged Campbell with questions about the activities and character of the agents but was consistently overruled on challenges from Carroll's attorney. Campbell insisted he didn't know why the freeholders refused to pay Guarantee's bill.

Wescott changed course, noting that of 188 indictments compiled by the agency, most originated from Wildwood. He predicted those cases would lose in court and that Campbell knew this and had refused requests for trials made by numerous accused violators. Wescott veered again, asking about "shakedowns" attempted by the operatives. He questioned their charged expenses.

Carroll used five men and two women, disguised as "flappers." Among their expenses charged to the county: hotel rooms, lunches, taxi fares, beer, cigars, tips, phone calls. Another expense, "girls," was explained. Flappers were young women hired by agents to go under cover with them while they made their setup purchases with suspected violators.

Ira Reeves, in his remembrance of his short term as New Jersey's Prohibition enforcement director, described the "rules of engagement" in making a liquor bust: The agent should actually buy and consume some liquid, determining it to be alcohol and the proprietor as selling same, before making a raid. "Purchase is evidence," according to Reeves.

Some smart barkeeps played the game. They wouldn't take money until they were satisfied the customer wasn't a fed. If they suspected, they'd return the money, thus invalidating the transaction.

This required agents to drink a lot on the job. Agents often "lit up" in the performance of their duly sworn duty. Inevitably, there were bad apples.

The unfortunately named Ralph Crooks was discussed. The former New York City cop had been arrested for allegedly purchasing liquor at hotels, then offering to destroy the evidence and provide "protection" for monetary consideration.

Colonel Ira Reeves in uniform. *Monmouth County Historical Society.*

While Guarantee's billings were adjudicated, Campbell's office became embroiled in another booze-related controversy: The Case of What to Do with the Confiscated Booze.

This time, the prosecutor was pitted against County Sheriff James Hoffman, with the freeholders again playing the role of penny-pinching government bureaucrats. Another bill lay at the center of the case, this one for $1,149.50, submitted by the sheriff's office to pay for a watchman, hired to guard 330 cases of liquor in county custody. These goods were seized a year earlier when a schooner ran aground at Higbee's Beach. The stock was valued at $10,000.

The sheriff blamed Campbell for the bill.

At the time, the county jail was being renovated. There was no space available to store evidence, like 330 cases of booze. It was kept in the cellar, unsecured, so it had to be watched. "We had information that someone planned to steal it," Hoffman noted.

Campbell had wanted it stored in a cell. Since the booze was evidence, it could not be destroyed until the matter was tried and a decision made about disposing of the liquor. In this situation, however, there never was a trial because the prosecutor couldn't find anyone to try. The crew of the schooner had abandoned ship. Its owner couldn't be found.

If the sheriff took it upon himself to destroy the booze, Campbell asserted, he'd be liable for its value.

CMCH sheriff residence, jail and courthouse postcard. *CHhistory.com.*

Campbell came in for criticism when Hoffman revealed the schooner's owner, Charles Beers of Atlantic City, had indeed been located but never indicted. Campbell argued that he lacked sufficient grounds to indict Beers. The sheriff disagreed.

The pair also clashed about the need for a watchman since room should have been made at the jail for the homeless liquor. Hoffman insisted the watchman was needed due to possibilities of theft, noting he'd personally been offered $1,500 to "look the other way."

Playing Solomon, County Solicitor Palmer Way suggested a way out of the dilemma: a formal petition to have the liquor destroyed. Campbell agreed, provided the sheriff signed the petition, which Hoffman declined to do, claiming the booze was of "too high a quality to simply destroy."

Hoffman suggested medicinal use. A chemist was summoned from Trenton to test the booze. Being 100 percent pure Belgian alcohol, it passed with flying colors. The liquor was subsequently distributed among a number of area hospitals, including Dr. Margaret Mace's Hospital in North Wildwood.

What about that unpaid watchman?

The grand jury agreed with Campbell. The bill was paid. The grand jury didn't want the matter entangled in "protracted litigation."

Hopefully, someone detected some irony in that.

***

Ludy Bishop no longer operated the business, but Anglesea Café was by no means dry. Agents proved that during a raid, arresting new proprietor Phillip Decorato for possession. He was fined $300. Otherwise, the liquor situation in Anglesea in 1927 was Saharan.

Coast Guardsmen commanded by Captain Charles Wright at nearby Hereford Inlet reported no recent captures but "constant vigilance." Recalling Rum Row's recent "glory years," Wright reminded the *Wildwood Journal Tribune* that thousands of cases of illegal liquor had been seized and temporarily stored at the inlet station and rum boats held under "lock and key at Anglesea Inlet."

"Not eliminated. But the running of rum has been so reduced as to make the amount landed negligible."

Not so, on the bayside.

In early February, the sheriff's office seized more than four hundred cases when a forty-five-foot cabin cruiser ran aground at Higbee's Beach, not far from Signal Hill, highest point in the area, said by locals to have once served as lookout spot for the pirate Captain Kidd. These days, the hill allegedly served as lookout point for smugglers working the bayside.

Crew having fled, no arrests were made. But the smugglers had stuck around long enough to hide treasure in the dunes, where authorities found another thirty-five cases of booze. Avoiding the earlier storage boondoggle at county jail, the sheriff stored this cache under lock and key at the county garage near his office.

Farther up the bay, state police caught rumrunners unloading 350 cases of whisky from a barge on West Creek onto a truck parked on a lonely stretch of swamp road. Cops confiscated the booze, the boat, the truck and an automobile. They arrested two men. The liquor had been packed in burlap, in 12-bottle lots. The bottles were marked "Old Log Cabin," "Golden Wedding" and "Black and White."

Anglesea's sea supply routes might have been cut by Captain Wright and his station, but Anglesea had other means of getting wet goods.

A tip from one lawbreaker against another brought raiders to the Penn Ice House, where they found twenty-two half barrels of high-powered beer along with thirty-seven barrels of less potent brew. A sample taken on the latter proved its alcohol content also exceeded legal limits, so the entire

Penn Ice, North Wildwood, New Jersey. *George F. Boyer Historical Museum.*

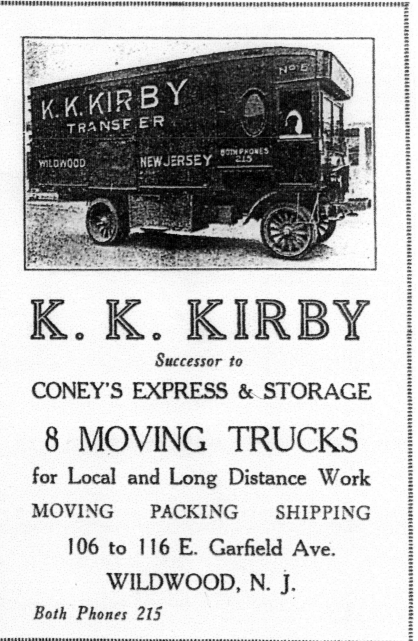

K.K. Kirby Express newspaper ad. *George F. Boyer Historical Museum.*

stock was hauled off to storage at county jail. The thirty-seven barrels of lower content beer belonged to local express man K.K. Kirby, who "defied conviction," according to the *Gazette*.

The grand jury seemed to agree, returning no indictment against Kirby because the prosecutor informed jurors that each of the seized barrels bore government certificates stating the beer was less than $\frac{1}{2}$ of 1 percent alcohol. Campbell asked that that portion of the seized beer be returned to storage at Penn Ice.

The court withheld decision pending further investigation as to whether the beer exceeded the legal limit or the certificates were fraudulent.

Meanwhile, Richard Coney, alleged owner of the higher octane brew, was indicted for possession. The questionable beer, tested by state chemists, proved to be a "trifle over the limit." Campbell persisted in pushing for its return to Kirby, but not without adding a warning. "If you move it [from Penn Ice], you'll be arrested for transportation." A real challenge to a man whose business was moving things.

Kirby argued the beer was the same "type" he'd legally shipped since enactment of Prohibition. He contended the slight increase in alcohol percentage occurred while the beer "aged" in storage. He suggested it would meet legal requirements if allowed to keep "on ice."

To brew near beer (under .5 percent alcohol), you first brew high-powered beer (4 percent or more alcohol). Remove the alcohol by freezing the beer until the alcohol level reaches the desired limit. That simple. Kirby was no chemist, but he knew his near beer.

The case was pended again, to hear from a brewing expert.

***

Needing a quote, newspapermen gathered, pencils ready. Law enforcement officials rolled their eyes in exasperation. Dry advocates cheered. Their wet adversaries jeered.

The Raiding Parson was back!

And John Adams had plenty to say.

The *New York Times* March 10 edition announced that Adams knew the names of five "prominent citizens of Cape May County" involved in rumrunning.

Speaking at a dinner in Ocean City, Adams intimated that booze was made and sold regularly in that bastion of Methodism and that "certain city officials" were in on it. He described Ocean City as a "haven for rumrunners and a gambling hole." In his earlier stint as Prohibition agent,

Adams's escapades carried him from Atlantic City to Cape May, so he claimed legitimacy as an expert in recognizing a den of iniquity when he raided one.

He questioned Ocean City's long cherished self-image as an oasis of temperance.

Ocean City police chief Howard Johnson, bristling at Adams's slur upon his city, demanded Adams prove his assertions. Mayor Joseph Champion dismissed the parson as a "fanatical prohibitionist, out for notoriety."

In 1926, Ocean City had experienced a mere twenty-four Volstead arrests

Nonetheless, Champion, perhaps chafing from the verbal lashing his city received from the raiding parson, promised to make Ocean City "cleanest in the state." He ordered police to create a "flying squadron" to discourage all vice within the city's boundaries. County Prosecutor William Campbell, an Ocean City lad, called Adams's bluff. He subpoenaed the parson to name names for the grand jury.

Headline-making revelations were expected. Smuggling empires teetered on the brink, ready to crumble once Adams expounded on the witness stand.

His appearance lasted all of six minutes.

No names revealed.

"I believe in the law," he offered, explaining his tendency to occasionally hyperbolize on the subject of booze.

In his speeches, he'd described in detail how liquor systematically flowed through Ocean City from points as far afield as Bivalve on Delaware Bay and, of course, Anglesea and Otten's Harbor. He seemed so sure of his information.

Testifying under oath before the Grand Jury, Adams clammed up. He denied knowing any specific law violators in Ocean City. He accused the media of misquoting him. He acted conciliatory toward the prosecutor, offering to assist officials charged with enforcing Volstead, "Without charging for my services."

Campbell might have had another reason for pressing Adams. Money. While the parson took shots at local law enforcement, Campbell pressed the freeholders for additional funds to try unresolved liquor cases arising from the summer of 1926's Guarantee Detective Agency arrest spree in Wildwood. Campbell wanted to dispose of those cases and requested an additional $600 to cover trial costs.

Apparently, one law enforcement official took Adams up on his offer of free help. The results, as headlined in the April 19 *Gazette*, were less than spectacular: "Promising Smuggling Revelation Proves Flop."

Based on information from Adams, authorities staked out the railroad for a night, waiting for a freight car loaded with booze bound for Wildwood. Adams had insisted the camouflaged goods would be deposited at Wildwood Junction.

The train arrived on schedule and departed for its next stop after being thoroughly searched. No liquor was on board. Adams offered an explanation. The bootleggers had learned he was on to them so they unloaded the goods at an earlier stop.

Plausible? Perhaps, but the law had quite enough of the parson's assistance, and Adams soon faded from the spotlight.

**

Friday, May 13, brought bad luck to the Hamburg Restaurant. Law enforcement made a big haul of 2,300 bottles of assorted liquor, including three gallons of wine, jugs of whisky, crocks filled with beer. In the cellar, over 800 bottles of booze hung on the wall. Another cache was buried in the yard behind the restaurant.

Federal raiders knew they'd always find action in Wildwood. Willard Barcus led a raid on Ye Olde Yacht Club on Hoffman Canal in North Wildwood. Three were arrested, including alleged proprietor Gardiner Moore and bartender Walt Larkin.

Agents claimed they were served highballs. They seized pints of whisky from the bar. Moore, Republican Party leader in North Wildwood, was released on $1,000 bail.

Barcus vowed to visit all parts of the county to "clean up the many establishments violating the law." He led raids on the Pacific Hotel, and owner Jonathan James was arrested. Barcus's method of operation was the same as at the yacht club. He purchased a drink, then arrested James and bartender Warner Corson.

Searching the hotel, agents found three gallons of alcohol and twenty-four pints of whisky.

A leading figure in county Democratic politics, James had previous experience with Volstead when Sheriff Hoffman raided the Pacific. On that occasion, James fought the case to the state supreme court. Due to a finding of defective warrant, the liquor was returned, but James was re-arrested for transporting it back to his hotel.

That case still had not been adjudicated when this arrest occurred, the *Leader* reported.

***

Reacting to complaints about young girls staggering out of Wildwood cabarets at dawn, the Wildwood Hotel Association urged the city to clean up the town. Its demand was echoed by the local chamber of commerce and Ministerial Union. They cited unrestricted sale of alcohol on the boardwalk as well as Sunday night dances at the piers, cabaret shows and sideshow barkers.

Prosecutor Campbell promised to act against violators.

With forces of law and order coalescing against them, the last thing Volstead violators needed was deception among their fellow "criminals." But wets in Wildwood experienced fraudulent beer as well as fraudulent enforcement agents.

The fake beer incident involved two men from Philly who sold K.K. Kirby 250 barrels of near beer. Kirby paid $1,150 for the goods in what should have been a clean, legal business transaction. Only the near beer wasn't even close to "near." When Kirby arrived at the train station to collect his merchandise, he discovered that he'd paid for 250 barrels filled with cardboard.

There was further duplicity from a pair of Philadelphians—perhaps the same pair who sold Kirby the goods—attempting to extract money from the proprietors of the Club Alabam in Anglesea. The duo posed as dry agents from "the Philadelphia office." They boasted of being confidantes of Mickey Duffy, notorious Philly hoodlum.

A fight broke out at the club, and the fake agents fled, the license plate on their car covered with cloth to avoid tracing. Cape May County had drawn the interest of the "official" criminal element.

The county had drawn attention of the resurgent Ku Klux Klan as well, with the *Gazette* reporting a "huge rally" at Stone Harbor featuring KKK Day Parade. Members marched in full sheeted regalia. An afternoon band concert followed.

The highlight of the all-day event was a lecture, "Why the KKK?" A crowd of five thousand from as far away as Virginia attended.

Kelly Kitko wasn't likely in attendance.

Identified as an "unnaturalized Polish immigrant" in the United States for twenty-four years, the jobless Kitko dwelled "somewhere in the woods near Goshen." Foreign. No permanent address. Unemployed. Spoke broken English...not exactly KKK material. And he made booze, too. White mule.

When he was arrested, Kitko had been drinking his own noxious brew. Witnesses described him as a raving maniac. A hot bath did wonders, Kitko's pores opened, poisonous vapors dissipated. He became a new man, entering the Cape May County Court of Common Pleas to face its new judge: Henry Eldredge, finally reappointed by Governor Harry Moore in April 1927. It had taken a year to get him back on the bench.

Kelly Kitko didn't care about that as he faced Eldredge on charges of manufacturing alcohol. "Just one time I try it," he explained in broken English, denying any wrongdoing. "I respectable citizen."

To prove it, he asked Eldredge to preside at his wedding. He planned to make an "honest woman" out of his live-in companion out in the woods of Goshen.

"But I don't speak Polish," Eldredge replied. The reason Bright opposed his reappointment revealed at last? Eldredge gave Kitko an early wedding present, dismissing the charges. No word on whether the respectable citizen married the girl.

***

Was the Raiding Parson right about that train after all? Law enforcement's sleepless night with Adams was repaid in late July when they seized fifty-two barrels of high-powered beer at Pennsylvania Railroad's Bennett Station at Erma.

Another Reverend John, this time Brewin, pastor of Erma Methodist Church, fetched the sheriff when he learned beer was being unloaded. Hoffman arrived to find men hauling barrels labeled "oats" from train car to trucks belonging to K.K. Kirby.

The remaining kegs on the truck were seized. The truck driver wasn't arrested because it "couldn't be shown that he had transported illegal beer." He was ordered to take his load to Court House where the beer was stored in the renovated county jail.

Subsequent tests performed on the oats showed 4 percent alcohol.

Judge Eldredge ordered it destroyed. The barrels were duly emptied into meadows along Stone Harbor Boulevard, having been transported to the site in a K.K. Kirby truck.

A crowd gathered by the meadow to silently mourn.

***

What of Rum Row? The twelve-mile limit, combined with the Coast Guard's improved firepower, had eliminated the "thrills and easy cash" of the early days of Prohibition.

Yet Colonel Ira Reeves, the state's latest director of Prohibition, was convinced it was making a comeback as 1927 entered its summer season. Smuggling increased along the coast, and the row showed signs of reviving. Not so, Admiral Billard assured the WCTU convention at Ocean Grove, describing the Coast Guard's blockade of the New Jersey coast as "stronger than that imposed by the Union against Confederacy."

"No more than 10 percent of the liquor of previous years gets through," Billard declared.

The addition of air power to existing forces at Cape May had drastically altered the playing field in favor of dry forces. Seaplanes from Station Nine conducted round-the-clock inspections of the coast. Secluded coves and deserted beaches were no longer "invisible" landing sites for smugglers.

In charge of this air force in 1927 was Chief Gunner C.T. Thrun, a pilot, and Ensign Walter Andersen. They used two types of plane, according to the *Wildwood Leader*, a seaplane with a 200-horsepower engine similar in design to Lindbergh's celebrated flying machine. It enjoyed a 350-mile cruising radius. The other plane was an OL5 amphibian. Both planes were equipped with radio and machine guns.

The base at Cape May had four hangars and a special building for a dirigible. In 1927, the Coast Guard further reinforced, adding seventy-five-foot patrol boats and manpower recently assigned to its operation.

Firepower aside, it was a tip from a "mysterious woman" that led to a rumrunner capture on November 11.

Registered out of Nova Scotia, the two-mast schooner *Eda and Charles* was captured, engines off and running without lights, while attempting to dock at Delaware breakwater under cover of fog and darkness.

Hidden beneath a load of coal was a $200,000 liquor cargo.

According to the tipster, smugglers planned to land the booze in time for the holiday season. The catch included three hundred barrels of malt and forty cases of assorted liquor, originating from the Great West Wine Company at St. Pierre, Miquelon. The French-owned island had, by 1927, replaced Nassau as the East Coast's primary source of European and Canadian liquor.

Seven were arrested, including Charles Brown, an alleged owner of the cargo.

And the mysterious woman? Rumor had it she belonged to a rival gang; always willing to help the Coast Guard hurt the competition.

Federal agents admiring their haul. *Temple University.*

For stats aficionados, the fiscal year through June 30 was good for law enforcement. Bootleggers lost $7.5 million, with $6.4 million of that destroyed. New Jersey was way ahead of other states, none of which exceeded $5 million.

Was New Jersey more efficient or did the state simply have more booze to deal with than anybody else?

Dodging the question, officials cited other impressive figures about the Garden State. Cost of operating the dry unit was $155,589 for the year, while Massachusetts, for example, paid more than $500,000 in salaries alone. Frugal New Jersey also spent the lowest amount for obtaining evidence.

But New Jersey also made the fewest arrests, 1,466, opposed to neighboring New York's 16,583. Bottom line of all the reports and columns of numbers: make the agencies look good and prove Prohibition an unabashed success.

Yet people still drank. And in some cases, drinking killed them.

***

Max "BooBoo" Hoff. *Temple University.*

It's natural at Christmas for families to want to be together. Larry West's wife was no exception. Problem was, West was wanted by the law. Tapping the wife's phone, Philly cops were able to track down West, hiding out in that city.

They arranged for Wildwood police chief Oakford Cobb to get his man. West was charged with involuntary manslaughter in the deaths of two men in Wildwood, where West owned a café on the boardwalk and a poolroom near Otten's Harbor.

The men who died were Seymour Gifford and Richard Ingham. The forty-two-year-old Ingham was a fish peddler working at the harbor. Realizing he was dying, Ingham whispered to his brother, Daniel, who was holding the dying man in his arms, the identity of the man who sold him the liquor that did him in.

Larry West.

A jury convened by Coroner Harry Hornstine submitted verdicts of involuntary manslaughter against West and the bartender who'd served the drinks.

Cause of death? Methyl alcohol poisoning.

Judge Eldredge sentenced West to four months in county jail for selling the poisoned liquor. The bartender drew a $500 fine. There's no record for fiscal year 1927 that includes the names Gifford and Ingham, but one figure from the report is relevant in light of their deaths.

New Jersey produced 13.6 million gallons of industrial alcohol during this period. More than twice as much as second-place New York. The Garden State was certainly an industrial center, but one wonders how much of that alcohol made its way to the street as illegal booze.

Industrial alcohol was produced with methanol added, as per the Volstead Act, a stipulation insisted upon by the powerful Anti-Saloon League. Being legal, industrial alcohol proved easily obtained by the criminal element and gained in popularity once Rum Row's demise dramatically reduced the flow of booze from foreign countries.

Max "Boo Boo" Hoff's Philadelphia syndicate was known to have re-distilled millions of gallons of the stuff for resale to the desperately thirsty.

It's not unlikely that some found its way to Wildwood and Larry West's pool hall.

1928

Colonel Ira Reeves served as New Jersey's director of Prohibition in 1927, resigning in frustration at the end of that year. Summarizing his year in office, Reeves lamented there were just as many bootleggers making bigger profits than ever. "Prohibition laws," he concluded "are unenforceable." He wrote a book about his experience, *Ol' Rum River*. In it, he enumerated what Prohibition did accomplish.

Took away people's say in making laws. Kept several hundred thousand honest citizens from working. Curtailed justice and honesty in the legal system and public office. Replaced good government with a "maze of slime, muck, graft, and corruption."

He offered a summary of Prohibition's costs for one year. Federal law enforcement: $40 million. Loss of federal revenue: $861 million. Loss of state and municipal revenue: $50 million. Adding that up equaled nearly 90 percent of what the nation paid in personal income tax, Reeves figured.

Reeves further enumerated increases in lawbreaking activity since 1920. For instance, in Prohibition's first year, 15,416 stills were seized. In 1928, that number rose to 216,611. In 1920, 153,735 gallons of liquor were seized. Eight years later, that amount ballooned to a staggering 32.5 million gallons. He added that the alcohol-related death rate since 1920 had increased by 317 percent.

Had Seymour Giffords and Richard Ingham made the stats after all?

And what did Ira Reeves accomplish in his year in office? In his own words, "Our efforts had raised the price of alcoholic beverage and reduced the quality."

New Jersey Prohibition director Ira Reeves. *Monmouth County Historical Society*.

***

Cutting one bottle of whisky created at least five bottles of rotgut. The most obvious additive was water. Assorted flavorings approximated taste and color.

A modified bottle of scotch was watered, then touched up with caramel or prune juice, even creosote. Finally, it was refortified with a jolt of legal and lethal industrial alcohol.

Industrial alcohol was used in making cleaning solutions and insecticides. The addition of methanol during Prohibition rendered the alcohol poisonous when taken internally. Bootleggers, especially organized crime elements, didn't care. Their sole concern was generating as much profit as possible as quickly as possible.

Other booze additives included rubbing alcohol, brake fluid, engine fuel, kerosene, shellac, sulfuric acid, camphor, formaldehyde, ether, perfume, hair tonic, iodine and antifreeze. Used antifreeze was especially popular because rust from radiators enhanced the color of the liquor.

Thanks to creative chemistry, deaths from poisoned alcohol reached a high of 4 per 100,000 in 1927, more than four times the 1920 rate. In the first week of 1928, William Hawkey of North Wildwood joined that group, killed from drinking wood alcohol. James Delany, also of North Wildwood, died in the same fashion a few days later.

North Wildwood mayor George Redding and police. *George F. Boyer Historical Museum.*

"Most of the liquor coming here is doctored," G.W. Knight, chief chemist of the Port of New York, told the *Public Ledger*. Knight analyzed booze samples, finding wood alcohol to be a major component. "Bootleggers use redistilled alcohol to increase profits," Knight explained.

Prior to Prohibition, the lab where imported liquor was tested needed one small cabinet to store samples awaiting testing. By 1928, several rooms of storage space overflowed.

The *Gazette* editorialized in January for government to increase efforts to stop "murder by bottle" by more effectively enforcing the law.

North Wildwood mayor George Redding took the editorial to heart. Meeting with police and other officials, Redding ordered police to stop and examine all cars driving onto the island, eliminating land access for bootlegged booze, hiring "special officers" for the job.

"Two men have died in North Wildwood," Redding stated. "It's up to us to stop any car carrying beer or liquor that is contrary to the law."

***

Wednesday became known as "Plea Day" in Judge Eldredge's courtroom, a chance for accused wrongdoers, mostly Volstead violators, to bargain with the judge.

Helen and John Applebee, from Dennisville, pleading guilty to charges of possession and maintaining a disorderly house, hoped their ages would work in their favor. John, seventy-five, paralyzed with a stroke, was unable to appear in court. His seventy-three-year-old spouse was described by her attorney as a "decent and respectable woman with an unblemished record."

While Helen watered the courtroom floor with penitent tears, her lawyer asked for suspended sentence, suggesting that jail time for the aged pair would be "barbarous treatment."

Despite testimony from the Applebees' neighbors in this close-knit rural community about "comings and goings from Applebee's of folk in all sorts of condition," the judge spared them. "But one more complaint from your neighbors and you'll be sent to jail," he said.

Eldredge also went easy on a pair of Rio Grande men, William Wheeler and George Durmont, fining each twenty-five dollars when they pleaded guilty to possession. Both asked for leniency, as they were "family men."

Prosecutor Campbell may have facilitated their generous treatment, pointing out that Wheeler had booze with no evidence of manufacturing

Main Street Dennisville, one of the larger towns in the county. *Dennis Township Museum.*

or selling it, while Durmont did have a still but there was no proof he was selling liquor. "If you sold the stuff," Eldredge informed both men, "I'd send you to jail for sixty days, despite your families."

Meanwhile, thirty-seven speakeasies were padlocked in Wildwood during the first week of February. This compared to forty-three padlockings during all of 1927.

Agents under Willard Barcus raided two familiar spots, the Elmira and Bradley Hotels, neighboring properties on Schellenger Avenue. Charles Bradley, alleged proprietor of both venues, was arrested. As for confiscated booze, it was slim pickings. Agents found two quarts at the Bradley, while the Elmira yielded a mere quart.

The Coast Guard continued to control area waters, making 1928 the quietest year at sea since the onset of Prohibition. However, there was some activity. A four-hundred-ton schooner eighteen miles off Townsend's Inlet appeared to be in difficulty, having encountered storms in its travels. Coast Guard hydroplanes spotted it during rounds from Cape May to Barnegat. A cutter was dispatched to investigate.

Upon reaching the schooner, the cutter's crew was greeted by taunts from the vessel. "We're bound for Sea Isle out of Nova Scotia with plenty of good liquor aboard. Want some?" Since the schooner remained beyond the twelve-mile limit, the cutter could do nothing but endure the jeering. And wait.

Sooner or later, the schooner had to make a move. It was in such bad shape it wouldn't remain seaworthy much longer, leaving its operator two options: make for safe docking at Sea Isle for repairs or try returning to Canada. If he chose the former, he'd have to jettison the cargo or face seizure. If the latter, the ship probably wouldn't make it.

A far cry from the heady days of Bill McCoy.

There's a footnote to the schooner story. Frank Widerstrom, captaining the fishing vessel *Victoria* out of Anglesea, came upon a derelict schooner shortly thereafter. Its sails badly tattered, the abandoned vessel drifted aimlessly. Widerstrom boarded. Finding no charts or identifying documents, the fisherman took it as his prize in keeping with long-held tradition of Jersey privateers. The Coast Guard intercepted him as he steamed home, schooner in tow.

Authorities seized the boat, thinking it the lost rumrunner. Widerstrom insisted the vessel belonged to him. He refused to leave his prize, staying on board while the Coast Guard towed the schooner to Atlantic City. They eventually identified the derelict as the *John L Martino* out of Baltimore.

But of its boozy secrets, no one ever learned more.

Back on shore, summer came and went in Wildwood. Willard Barcus's padlocking raids had produced a quiet season. The biggest Volstead story of summer 1928 involved a fishing boat that left Otten's Harbor to go fishing and returned with a load…of fish.

The fishing smack *Riverside* pulled in to Cold Spring Inlet, headed for the processing plant at Richardson Sound, scene of previous liquor-related activities. Apparently tipped off that skullduggery was afoot, the Coast Guard swarmed aboard to search for booze. By the time they finished and released the boat, tides had shifted and the *Riverside* was stranded in mud, unable to reach docking. The boat sat, waiting for the incoming tide to raise it up.

A crowd gathered near Rio Grande Boulevard wharf to watch the unloading party, anticipating illegal delights. But in the end, after all the waiting…it was just a fish story. Fishing was a major industry during the 1920s, but even then records showed declining catches from previous decades.

In 1926, according to the *Cape May County Gazette*, New Jersey fisheries employed almost ten thousand, a decline from 1921 of nearly 5 percent. Catch totals amounted to 168 million pounds, valued at $12.4 million.

Waiting at the dock at Anglesea. *George F. Boyer Historical Museum.*

Significant numbers, but still lower than 1921, with the catch dropping a drastic 50 percent.

The Federal Bureau of Fisheries attributed the decline not to lucrative distractions like rumrunning but to overfishing. Commercial methods were depleting most "valuable" fish stocks. The bureau took action—it initiated a study.

What were the optimum amounts that could be harvested without wiping out species? There was no talk one hundred years ago of applying quotas such as those in place now. But studies continue to this day.

***

The county's annual WCTU convention, held in Stone Harbor, boasted its largest turnout in its history. The organization was "well-fixed financially" and pledged to work "aggressively to elect temperance candidates" in the coming election.

In 1928, Herbert Hoover was elected president on a promise to stay the course on pretty much everything, including Prohibition. New Jersey voters must have been thinking dry this election. They chose their first Republican governor in nine years, Morgan Larson. Dry Hamilton Kean went to the U.S. Senate, replacing Edward Edwards. The popularity of "Wet as the Atlantic Ocean" had dried up at the polls.

But the state remained damp otherwise.

State and local authorities raided Rose Bud Café in Cape May, seizing 1,036 bottles of beer and 1½ pints of hard liquor, along with 50 gallons of mash. Willard Barcus led raiders to the Cliff House, where they busted the county's first drive-through speakeasy. Three customers were arrested as they drove up, paid a waiter five dollars for pints of whisky, then sat with cars running while the goods were fetched.

Cape May's Nick Buganis was jailed for sixty days for maintaining a "nuisance house." Over one thousand bottles of beer and one of whisky

Industrial alcohol jar found in the woods. *Dennis Township Museum.*

were destroyed. In addition to selling alcohol, Buganis was sentenced for allowing men and women to "assemble for gaming purposes."

Two interesting cases were described in local papers toward the end of 1928. The first involved Avalon justice of the peace Charles Wood. Wood was arrested when his wife charged the sixty-three-year-old man with assault after he beat her while "under the influence." Wood pleaded guilty.

Wood had obtained his booze from Avalon poolroom owner Peter Vasselo. Vasselo had been coincidentally fined $200 for possession after a raid on his premises. Wood claimed he'd purchased grape juice. That fib earned him an indictment for perjury. Vasselo paid Wood's bail, expecting "pay back" from the justice of the peace in his own case. Wood subsequently testified that he'd given false testimony because he was "confused and mentally upset after being arrested."

Avalon mayor Gus Bergner interceded on Wood's behalf, asking the court for leniency. Sleuths searching the pool hall found two fifteen-gallon kegs of moonshine and two thirty-gallon kegs of Italian red wine. Judge Eldredge suspended Wood's sentence.

Temporary insanity plea modified to temporarily addled?

The second case involved a DUI arrest magistrates didn't want to adjudicate. The arresting constable first brought the accused to Stone Harbor's justice of the peace, who refused to handle the matter. "The man could walk straight as an arrow," J.P. Herbert assessed, uninterested.

The accused was then brought to Wildwood's John O'Farrell, who "wasn't available." Stone Harbor mayor George Markland finally dismissed the case, extracting five dollars for a doctor's exam.

Witnesses claimed the driver sped through "stop" signs, accompanied by a "nearly naked woman" who offered "choice epithets to bystanders." She had been arrested as well.

County Medical Examiner D. Julius Way examined the driver, declaring him "moderately under the influence."

The *Gazette* editorialized the slapdash handling of the matter: "In light of developments of the past week, some of our justices of the peace need to be reminded that 'under the influence' doesn't necessarily mean 'drunk.'…Squires should remember that a physician's certificate is sufficient proof to warrant fining a driver on a charge of being under the influence."

Perhaps anticipating dryer times with Hoover in office, enterprising moonshiners in the Pines around Woodbine designed, built and concealed a still capable of cooking five hundred gallons of booze at a time.

Located several miles from the nearest road, a cedar log cabin incorporated pipes concealed with pine branches in ground, roof and entry and ventilation. The cabin contained nine barrels of fermenting mash. Authorities dismantled the still, destroying its contents. Its owner was never found.

1929

In 1929, Pauline Sabins, rich, articulate, attractive and Republican, assumed a leading role in the Women's Organization for National Prohibition Reform, which challenged the ASL, demanding changes to Prohibition laws. She was joined by wealthy friends, many eyeing a tax on legal booze, relief from the growing burden of the income tax.

"When woman entered the fight for repeal, sanity began to return to the country," observed Al Smith, losing Democratic candidate in the '28 presidential election.

In 1929, Americans drank more than when the great dry experiment began.

According to John Kobler's book *Ardent Spirits*, people guzzled 700 million gallons of home fermented wine between 1925 and 1929. That's three times more than the equivalent time period prior to Prohibition. That figure didn't include wines made from non-grape sources (cherries, apples). Home wine-making supply businesses surged, creating a $200 million industry.

Canadian distillers didn't fare poorly either. In 1921, Canada exported 8,335 gallons of whisky to the United States. By the end of 1928, thanks in large part to the proximity of French-owned islands St. Pierre and Miquelon, launching sites for East Coast smugglers, that total surpassed 1.1 million gallons.

Beer drinkers carried their share of the load. Home brewing demand consumed 900 million pounds of malt syrup in one year alone. Enough to produce 7 billion pints. Home brewers forked over $135 million for supplies needed to produce stove-top beer to guzzle with bathtub gin. Malt products were easily purchased in Piggly-Wiggly and other chain groceries of the era. Another 175,000 "specialty" outlets opened, specifically catering to the "hobby."

Even with increased "home-based" production, coupled with Coast Guard successes combatting Rum Row, booze smuggling into Cape May County persisted. As Prohibition's first decade concluded, focus of illegal activity shifted from ocean to bayside. The battle was taken up by state and local law enforcement, sometimes in seeming competition with their federal counterparts.

In early 1929, new County Sheriff Forrest Rich didn't waste time posting his name on the booze bust scoreboard. Leading a combined county-state task force raid on an area known as Lincoln farm, Rich seized five hundred cases of imported liquor and twenty-eight barrels of mash valued at $75,000. Five men were arrested. Raiders confiscated machine guns, rifles and pistols along with ammunition.

"A veritable arsenal," according to the sheriff.

Rich speculated the weapons belonged to a major smuggling ring that had been getting its goods from ships landing loads along both county shorelines. This haul included 175 cases of champagne, 50 of Bacardi rum, 100 crème de menthe, 50 dozen bottles of scotch, 150 cases of rye and 50 of Irish whisky.

An anonymous tip directed raiders down a rarely traveled road between Millville and Wildwood. There they captured both the truck and hapless lookout stationed to watch for trouble. Authorities confronted two men who attempted to draw weapons. They later claimed they believed they were being hijacked.

Investigators found liquor about a mile from the road. At least one loaded truck managed to get away. Police needed three trucks to haul away the contraband. They pursued and arrested three men, while seven others escaped into the woods. One of the three captured carried an automatic rifle, "loaded and ready for action," according to Rich.

Rich learned the liquor had been landed at nearby Sluice Creek. Bail was posted by John Martino, a Beeseley's Point property owner. Because the men were arrested away from the spot where the liquor was found, Court Commissioner George Greis did not hold them on possession charges.

Two weeks later, authorities captured an Atlantic City man, said to have been one of the seven who fled the night of the raid. Bail bond in his case was posted by a man the *Leader* described as a "well-known resident of Five Mile Beach," without naming him.

The first three men called to trial—Louis Nathanson, Abe Levin and Charles Goodleman—pleaded not guilty through Wildwood attorney Harry Tenenbaum. The booze was tested by a state chemist, found to be of medicinal quality and distributed to ten area hospitals as well as the county almshouse.

Meanwhile, raiders enjoyed success uncovering stills operating in the Woodbine area. State police hit Harry Kazan's farm in February, finding two stills producing twelve to twenty-five gallons along with ten gallons of finished moonshine, all stored in a barn. Kazan also had eighteen gallons of mash in the works.

Kazan claimed the liquor was for personal consumption. He allegedly offered arresting officers $300 to "forget being here." Bribery was added to manufacture and possession charges.

Such was the structure of New Jersey's legal system during Prohibition that Kazan faced two preliminary hearings. The bribery charge was heard by a justice of the peace in Cape May Court House. Kazan was then taken to

Typical Woodbine-area chicken farm. *Sam Azeez Museum of Woodbine Heritage.*

Cape May, where U.S. Commissioner Lewis Stevens dealt with the Volstead violations. Kazan didn't do very well in either venue, with bails imposed of $2,000 and $2,500, respectively.

State police also discovered a still operating in the woods near Dennisville. Julius Froelich, sixty-eight, admitted ownership and was charged with manufacturing and owning an "illegal utensil." He also had a quantity of mash but no finished liquor, so no possession charge was filed. Froelich, a repeat offender, had bail set at $2500.

A few weeks later, his son-in law Harry Moore was nabbed by troopers for possession and transportation. Quart bottles of liquor were found in his car. Moore tried smashing the evidence, doing in three jugs before officers stopped him. He eventually pleaded guilty and was fined $250 by Judge Eldredge.

Raiders maintained their active pace in the county's rural areas as winter thawed into spring. Moonshiners hoped to operate unnoticed.

Ignatz Kischak was noticed. Unfortunately for Ignatz, it was the third time he'd been noticed. Three strikes meant out, or rather in, as in jail. Kischak drew a six-month sentence and $500 fine after pleading guilty to possession of home brew. Raiders captured a fifteen-gallon-capacity still to go along with three gallons of brew.

A familiar name was listed among county sleuths joining the raiding party. Charles Umfreed had returned to his job as county detective. With former county clerk T. Millett Hand taking charge in the prosecutor's office from William Campbell in 1929, Umfreed was welcomed back.

T. Millet Hand, county prosecutor and future U.S. congressman. *Cumberland County Historical Society.*

Ignatz wasn't the only big catch on this occasion. Raiders also finally caught "the bee man."

Frank Skipalo was Kischak's neighbor. They lived in an area known as the Ludlam tract, probably so named for the first white settler in the area, Joseph Ludlam. Located near Woodbine in the vicinity of Great Cedar Swamp, it was mostly scrub pine and marsh, not easily accessed. Few lived here, eking out subsistence livings from the land.

Skipalo, known as "bee man" because he produced and sold honey, made ends meet with a forty-gallon underground still. The bee man first denied the still was his, claiming he didn't know it was on his property. He'd been under suspicion for four years and was previously raided. But this time the arrest was made, since Umfreed found the still operating.

Skipalo's still was built inside a dugout cave, five hundred square feet. The log ceiling was covered with sand, leaves and moss, the exterior disguised as a brush pile. Ventilation pipes extended underground some distance, camouflaged to resemble rabbit holes at the openings. Raiders found seven barrels of mash and several barrels of finished liquor in bee man's hive.

The innovative Skipalo was fined $500 by Judge Eldredge. Upon sentencing, bee man buzzed, gesticulating wildly, according to the *Gazette*, "shouting in Bohemian." He insisted he could pay only $100 but managed to gather the stipulated amount when Eldredge informed him he'd be jailed otherwise.

An apparently chastened bee man departed, vowing to stick to his "wife, daughter, and hives" and leave the moonshining to others. In another time, Skipalo might be a celebrated designer of distilleries or microbreweries. Instead, his still was dismantled and removed, his cave reduced to its natural state.

Tuckahoe road house operator William Fisher also pleaded guilty to possession charges and was fined $300. A raid by county detectives turned up seven cases of high-powered beer. Fisher was dimed out by a North Wildwood woman who complained to authorities that her husband frequently stopped at Fisher's, apparently for more than one for the road.

Having already sold his business and relocated, Fisher was spared a stay in county jail.

Millet Hand's work was cut out for him. The state's judicial district rated below national averages for both percentage of convictions obtained and proportion of jail time given to convicted violators (22 percent lower than national average).

Transfer of the Prohibition Bureau from Treasury to Justice, passage of the Jones Act and new President Hoover's inquiry into the state of Prohibition, the so-called Wickersham Commission, along with increased federal aid, were all directed at improving performance of the enforcement machinery to obtain heavier fines and longer sentences.

According to a U.S. Senate committee study of conditions in New Jersey, prosecutorial effectiveness in these areas was considered a "farce" as late as 1929. Hand had been handed a tough job.

Yet imbibe they did. Supplies continued flowing into the state from without and within. Local and state authorities continued to plug dikes, only to find themselves short on fingers.

State police made a big grab near Wildwood Golf Club, capturing six men, two trucks, a car and $60,000 worth of booze. The crew had obtained their supplies from a rumrunner who'd managed to evade the Coast Guard, landing his merchandise at Cold Spring Inlet.

Acting solo, trooper Andrew Zapolsky waited in ambush at a "lonely spot" along Shore Road and captured one truck unaided. His partner Nuncio Gaetano matched the feat. The troopers unloaded the trucks at Cape May Court House headquarters and then headed to Raymond Bailey's place in Cold Spring, where they'd learned the rest of the liquor had been cached. On the way, they intercepted the convoy car containing two armed men, whom they disarmed and arrested.

The captured trucks contained five hundred sacks of liquor, concealed behind twenty-five barrels of fish in each truck. The arrested Wildwood men gave addresses around Otten's Harbor. They were arraigned before Commissioner Douglas and held on $2,500 bail. Property owner Bailey was also arrested, though he claimed no knowledge that the lessors of his property were rumrunners.

Owner of the trucks K.K. Kirby posted $10,000 bonds for release of each truck and also posted bond for the four Wildwood men. Kirby claimed he'd rented the trucks but did not disclose the identity of his customer. Judge Eldredge eventually fined the four men a total of $1,100 after they pleaded guilty to possession and transportation.

Palmer Way, representing the four, sought and received a lighter fine for William Johnson, who'd revealed the hiding place of the liquor and helped troopers unload the truck.

The court picked up additional money from the Otten's Harbor area when Eldredge fined Joe Mekis and Beltranis Ulaucyus $300 for various liquor violations. Both owned establishments on the harbor. Both entered guilty pleas in exchange for lighter sentences. Beltranis had forty-two cases of home brew, Mekis thirty-two cases. The former was also charged with obstructing an officer.

County Detective Umfreed teamed up with local police on another late spring foray to the harbor area, finding more beer at Michael Balkan's place. The raid was in response to numerous complaints from a North Wildwood woman that her husband over-frequented Balkan's establishment.

Was she the same woman whose husband frequented Fisher's roadhouse at Tuckahoe? If so, authorities should have recruited her. She was obviously a relentless sleuth.

More activity at Otten's occurred, with police raiding Nora Hansen's boardinghouse. Mother and sole support of six children, Nora was "let off" with a $200 fine after pleading guilty in August of running a "disorderly house." Not counting those six kids. Nora explained she "had to provide liquor for her boarders or they wouldn't stay at her place."

The Otten's Harbor area along Park Boulevard, east to New Jersey Avenue, had long been home to Wildwood's minority and less affluent residents. A well-established black community flourished in the vicinity for many years. This community was not exempted from the temptations or legal travails associated with Prohibition.

George "Big Mose" Caldwell was well known throughout the island. Described by the *Leader* as "ebon hued," Caldwell was arrested in 1929 for possession of a small quantity of liquor. Appearing before superior court commissioner Robert Bright, Caldwell was bailed out by Ludy Bishop, another well-known local.

Asked his occupation, Caldwell indicated he operated a "soup kitchen." True enough. Caldwell was known to provide free soup for the area's needy during cold winter months. Perhaps he paid for his largesse with proceeds earned from selling a bit of liquor during warmer seasons.

Harry Tenenbaum, representing Big Mose, entered a guilty plea for possession in exchange for dropping the "selling" charge. Testifying for the prosecution, Doris Bradway "suspected Caldwell of being a law breaker." According to the *Leader*, Bradway "sent her colored maid to Caldwell's establishment with a dollar.

The maid reappeared, minus the dollar but holding a bottle of "something white." Bradway immediately turned over the evidence to the prosecutor.

Based on newspaper accounts, one can't help suspecting everyone living near Otten's Harbor was arrested at least once during Prohibition. While the harbor provided plenty to keep authorities busy, there was activity elsewhere.

Telphine Francesconi of Cape May was sentenced to six months in jail and a $500 fine for her third conviction. This time it was for possession. Her prior was for selling. "It's common knowledge that she's a bootlegger," Hand told the court. Eldredge reminded Telphine that he'd warned her last time she appeared before him that she'd be jailed for a third offense. He didn't disappoint.

Telphine ran what old time saloon habitués called a "blind tiger." The *Leader* clarified. A blind tiger "sold liquor secretly at prices below those prevailing at legitimate saloons, typically in seedier parts of town."

Blind tigers were also said to dispense the very cheapest rotgut liquor. "Rankest poison" insisted the *Leader*.

Telphine's product lived down to that standard. Selling it at twenty-five cents a drink at what from the outside appeared to be a grocery store; she concealed her liquor in tin vessels, easy to spill out in the event of a raid or dipped out to paying customers.

"Its prolonged containment in tin vessels added a level of toxicity," according to the newspaper.

Eldredge didn't care about sordid details. He pulled this tiger's teeth.

In Sea Isle, Lisa Mazzenelli, alleged owner of a home speakeasy, drew a crowd. State police, county detectives, Sheriff Rich and Sea Isle City police chief Charles Polak all squeezed into her premises. But she wasn't there. In her absence, they found five-gallon jugs of wine and whisky along with bottles of food coloring and a supply of empty bottles waiting to be filled with the product of Lisa's domestic chemistry.

A widow, she got by keeping boarders—and doctoring cheap moonshine to pass for quality liquor.

A rare moment of levity ensued later at the sheriff's office, when Rich, securing evidence seized at Lisa's place, inadvertently dropped a jug, spilling its contents. More than one officer instantly dropped to his knees, pantomiming the act of slurping vino from the floor.

***

The job of Prohibition director in New Jersey was no laughing matter. Edwin Ross, director in 1929, was the twelfth man to hold the title since Prohibition's inception in 1920.

And Ross was getting out.

"This job is enough to wear out anybody in a year," Ross's boss, Prohibition Commissioner James Doran, observed. Ross confirmed

Newly sworn Prohibition directors gather in D.C. *Mark Herron.*

Doran's comment...almost. He lasted eleven months. The average tenure was nine and a half months.

The first director, James Edgerton, friend of William Jennings Bryan, organized the unit. He stayed three months. Schoolteacher George Van Note was next. He toiled fourteen months before declaring his unit "so corrupt he could have taken $1 million without anyone noticing."

Quaker Charles Brown took over and hired Theodore "Two Gun" Schweitzer and his "rough and tumble" approach to enforcement. Brown resigned in December 1922. William Moss didn't let any grow under himself, coming and going before they could change the names on the office doors.

He was followed by Adrian Chamberlin, who conducted almost five thousand raids in a single year, 1924. But drys never took to his political connection with wet Senator Walter Edge. Chamberlin left on July 1, 1925.

Reuben Sams from Philadelphia lasted a month.

Colonel Ira Reeves took over in late 1926. He departed in May 1927, with enough negative material to write a book denigrating the entire idea of Prohibition. Reeves complained he'd been "heckled out of office."

Rueben Sams, in charge of Prohibition in southern New Jersey. *Mark Herron.*

Deputy Commissioner James Jones followed, with the idea of performing fewer, larger raids. His idea met with little success. Colonel Arthur Hanlon took charge after a month. Hanlon persevered fourteen months, failing to instill his military-type system of discipline and secrecy in charges.

Ross came aboard in October 1928.

***

Summer arrived in Wildwood. Flying squadrons of cops, troopers and detectives staged a Sunday raid on seven speakeasies. Ordered by Prosecutor Millet Hand, raiders filled a truck with whisky, wine and beer collected door to door on their rounds.

Charles Umfreed led the county contingent. Chief Cobb headed the Wildwood group. They hit Dock Street at Otten's Harbor. At Nora Hansen's place, they seized fifty nine-gallon barrels of home brew "working." Trooper Zapolsky, leading state police a few doors down, arrested Viola Nelson, who was "working" as well. Six men were arrested along with her. All were Wildwood men, giving addresses along Dock Street. Steps away, authorities busted Mike Balten's speakeasy. On Park Boulevard, they grabbed another speak operator, Theodore Wysywanik.

Going back the opposite side of Dock Street, dry forces dropped in at Dew Drop Inn, arresting Joe Mekis along with eight patrons. Gus and Pete, Vic and Fred…local lads off the boats looking for a little taste.

Marty Dubin, alias "Woodruf," was nabbed at the next stop, along with six others, one of whom listed his address as "Piggie," a boat docked at the harbor.

Raiders hit Ulaucyus again. This time, they avoided the lead pipe he kept handy to skull crack coppers the way he did the first time he was raided. Four more patrons were hauled in, along with the day's first female non-working girl, Nora Guy.

Cases of beer, gallon jugs of wine, concoctions of malt and hop in various stages of fermentation were seized. Home brew in bottle and barrel, bushel baskets filled with jars of joy juice and half-gallon containers of moonshine were confiscated.

Patrons were fined five dollars apiece. Owners paid more dearly. All that liquor was hauled away to county jail in the five-ton truck. Briefly, then, all was quiet in Wildwood. Very briefly.

Raiders visited the east side the following week. Sheriff Rich and Chief Cobb directed an official whirlwind down one side of Schellenger Avenue and up neighboring Cedar Avenue. They hit three places simultaneously, reducing the likelihood of warning spreading of their coming. Cobb's contingent raided the Hotel Blackstone, scoring five gallons of whisky, quarts and pints of rye and fifteen gallons of unspecified alcohol. They arrested owner Thomas Daigainas, who eventually pleaded guilty to possession.

Meanwhile, another group visited the familiar Hotel Bradley, where they confiscated a quantity of pints of whisky and made more arrests. Directly behind the Bradley, across a narrow alley, the Hotel Hamlet yielded no booze, but raiders startled one very unalert Paul Revere who ran shouting "state police" throughout the building only to find himself face to face with a contingent of same.

Authorities lit up a cigar store, arrested Ludy Bishop and Cliff Calhoun and broke up some gambling action. They also nabbed Harry Betts, owner of Hereford Hotel in Anglesea, along with twenty-six patrons. The three principals were held on bail. Patrons were fined five dollars each.

Finished with Wildwood for the time being, Rich headed north to Ocean City. An unusual number of raids were conducted throughout 1929 on that city's west side.

"It seemed like they were concentrating on the black neighborhood," Ocean City historian Fred Miller recalled. "Every time an Ocean City raid was reported in the papers, it was on West Avenue." This occasion was no exception.

The West Avenue disorderly house of Cora Cooper yielded a gallon of moonshine and a tearful plaintiff for Judge Eldredge's court. The *Gazette* described her tear-streaked face and "buxom figure convulsing" as she claimed she was a victim of "politics and jealousy." Four liquor violations and a disorderly house. Politics?

"They hounded me 'cause I wouldn't vote the Democrat ticket," she explained. Pleading not guilty, she chagrinned her attorney, admitting she sold "just a little liquor…to get along." Eldredge sentenced her to get along to county jail for sixty days.

Upon release, Cora abandoned Ocean City for Asbury Park, her jail time presumably inspiring a new lease on life. Or at least a change in venue.

***

The stock market crashed in October, the economy reeling nationwide. October was "off season" at the Jersey shore. Business was slow to nonexistent in the tourism industry. Effects of the downturn wouldn't be felt locally until the following summer.

Local drinkers experienced depression of a different kind as the Roaring Twenties closed.

The *Daisy T*, a forty-five-foot rum boat, was discovered in Delaware Bay, floating battered and abandoned in a channel off Cape May Point.

Daisy T was of the latest design, a twelve-cylinder engine speed boat with twin holds, fore and aft. Below deck contained another two holds. Airtight bulkheads kept her afloat. Her fore hold was filled with 125 sacks, each containing bottles of champagne, whisky and other choice brands. The cargo was removed by customs agents from Port of Philadelphia.

The story shrouded in mystery, locals whispered rumors of pirates—after all, these waters were said to have been frequented by Blackbeard and Captain Kidd. No one ever learned more about the *Daisy T*.

At the north end of the county, Great Egg Harbor separates Cape May from Atlantic County. Here, another story unfolded at the end of 1929. Coast Guard patrols captured a speedy launch bearing $100,000 worth of foreign liquor, a bust so large, officials crowed about finally breaking a long-suspected South Jersey–based smuggling operation.

A three-man crew grounded the launch near Ocean City Yacht Club, where they leaped ashore and escaped. The cargo of liquid delights was brought to Philly, joining the haul from *Daisy T*.

Stories mentioned Boo Boo Hoff, known Philly boxing promoter and reputed king of that city's illegal liquor rackets. Hoff reportedly owned properties in both Wildwood and Ocean City and a large tract on the mainland, not far from Great Egg Harbor. But there was no proof connecting Hoff to the incident.

No one knew for sure who was behind local smuggling operations.

That would wait for a new decade to sort out.

1930

By 1930, a growing number of Americans felt Prohibition wasn't working and government efforts to stop people from drinking were futile. Resources committed to dry programs could be better used to help people deal with the economic crisis gripping the nation.

A 1930 poll of 4.8 million people, conducted by *Literary Digest*, revealed that 30.5 percent favored staying the dry course, 29 percent favored modifications allowing beer and wine and 40.5 percent wanted to eliminate Prohibition laws altogether.

The National Economic League asked members to list four "paramount" problems facing the nation entering the new decade. In order, they listed: administration of justice, disrespect for the law, organized crime, inability of law enforcement to keep up with criminals. Translated to the root cause of those problems: Prohibition.

The American Bar Association, whose members benefitted from the increased need for legal services, polled 2–1 against Prohibition. Organizations originally supporting passage of the Eighteenth Amendment, including the American Legion, VFW and American Federation of Labor, now favored repeal.

Even John D. Rockefeller, once the single largest financial backer of the ASL, had changed his mind on the issue.

In Cape May County, the decade opened with the roar of engines at Sunset Lake near Otten's Harbor as two Coast Guard vehicles sped to a wharf where they captured the fifty-foot sloop *Margaret A*, loaded with six hundred cases of assorted liquor, valued at $40,000. Some of the stock had been dropped at nearby Wildwood Yacht Club.

Members of the rum crew had beaten a hasty retreat by the time the law arrived, but the sloop was later identified as belonging to Gottlieb Anderson of Wildwood.

The rumrunners had evaded capture at sea, despite being fired upon by a cutter, the *Leader* reported. Racing without running lights to avoid spotters, the sloop headed to Sunset Lake via Cold Spring Inlet, the crew apparently intending to unload onto waiting trucks before guardsmen stationed at Holly Beach could reach the scene.

But the Holly Beach men, under Captain Jesse Hearon, not only captured them running away from the dock but also discovered one hundred cases stowed in a nearby garage. Parked inside was likely transport for the goods, a truck owned by John Russo, owner of the Brass Rail near Otten's Harbor.

The booze, bottled in pints and quarts, was wrapped in corrugated paper and packed inside burlap bags. Labels identifying the packets as belonging to a Canadian firm were stamped "government certified" for medicinal use by a Detroit testing company.

While the Coast Guard investigated *Margaret A*, land officials continued their crackdown in Wildwood, again focusing near the harbor. State, county and local law hit likely speaks along Dock Street, while a second group returned to Cedar Avenue in the center of town. Officers visited Harry Morgan's Oyster House, seizing pints of whisky and cases of home brew.

Men working the west side under Oakford Cobb raided Theodore Johnson and neighbor Peter Tyne, alias "Moonshine Pete." They found booze at both locations. Johnson identified himself as "Terrible Turk," a former circus strong man then earning his living on the boardwalk, pulling automobiles by a rope clenched in his teeth. He also lifted "fat women" single-handed. Moonshine Pete's establishment was fitted out with a network of hoses connected to barrels containing liquids in various stages of fermentation.

Leaving that circus in custody, authorities proceeded to William Hickey's on Railroad Avenue, where they made a bigger score: seventeen barrels and six cases of high-powered beer. Cops returned the next day, raiding Russo's Brass Rail and Michael Donnelly's Central Inn. These hits netted a truckload of wines, beers and whisky.

A total of twenty-two places were raided, including Penn-Wood Hotel, Victor Café, Rocco Turchi's, Hamlet Hotel, Henie Hotel, Little Club Café, Ocean View Fish Market, Royal Hotel, Walnut House and Billy's Café.

Cape May wasn't totally ignored. Authorities also hit the Sea-View Inn near Schellenger's Landing.

Pursuing their pledge to make Wildwood as "dry as the Sahara Desert," law enforcement staged two more raids in the days immediately following. They hit Club Café, arresting owner Adam Kosobucki and finding a small supply of booze. Last but not least, they surprised Albin Carnevale at his Italian American grocery store. Raiders collected Carnevale's inventory of wine jugs, crocks of beer and a fifteen-gallon barrel of red.

Cape May County welcomed the 1930s.

***

The opening court session of 1930 witnessed the largest crowd of defendants gathered together at one time in all Henry Eldredge's years on the bench. The *Gazette* noted that not all the cases were Volstead based. Elements of the county populace conducted a crime spree to start the new decade. Burglary, robbery, larceny, assaulting officers, embezzlement, desertion and non-support were some of the issues the judge adjudicated.

But there was plenty of alcohol action as well.

Judge Eldredge sentenced Phillip Katz to $500 for keeping a disorderly house in Woodbine. George Lawton of Ocean City drew $250 for transporting booze in his car, though he claimed he didn't know it was there until police found it for him. Lewis Compare of Wildwood Crest drew jail for thirty days and a $500 fine as a repeat liquor offender. Compare had asked for clemency based on his having a wife, three children and no job. Eldredge offered an alternative solution: ship him back to his native Italy. North Wildwood's Giacomo Matera was arrested for operating a still and all the fixings at his store. He drew a $500 fine.

Charles White from Higbee's Beach was arrested by state troopers for making white mule. White's wife, Mary, was arrested when she tried disposing of gallons of white mule being taken as evidence. Making it a family affair, son Ellsworth was arrested for driving without a license. White drew sixty days for possession, and Ellsworth received thirty days for "conspiracy," while Mary got off easy with a ten-dollar fine. She'd done her sixty days for a previous offense.

Eldredge might well have worried about overcrowding the jail, because his workday wasn't finished.

Joe Collins, age seventy-three, destitute and crippled with rheumatism, contended his "condition" forced him to sell liquor to make ends meet.

Raiders found two barrels of mash upstairs at his place along with a still, keg of alcohol and supply of empty bottles. Instead of jail, Eldredge ordered Collins to the county almshouse.

Eldredge reduced jail population by one, releasing Ignatz Kischak. Three-time Volstead offender, the Woodbine man had been incarcerated since October for having three gallons of moonshine.

"Except for the church, no organization has done more for humanity than the WCTU," Eldredge exhorted a gathering of one hundred women at the county chapter's 1930 Spring Institute. "Whether organized crime is stronger than organized government is your problem and mine." He decried "so-called respectable citizens who sow seeds of confusion among society" by violating liquor laws. The guilt of bootleggers also rests with consumers who buy from them, Eldredge asserted.

That was music to the ears of WCTU. The attendance roster read like a who's who of old Cape May County with names like Rutherford, Gandy, Leaming, Sheppard, Hand and Corson at this "Christian Citizenship" conference. They were told that alcohol consumption was down 85 percent from pre-Prohibition years. They called for more stringent enforcement of the law.

Was Eldredge campaigning for a new job? The county bar association unanimously supported his promotion to the Circuit Court. He was confirmed swiftly by the state senate, after fifteen years as common pleas judge.

His seat on that bench went to Palmer Way of Wildwood.

***

As Prohibition proceeded, lawbreakers continued devising ingenious ways of circumventing the law, compelling authorities to play catch up. This was especially true of the Coast Guard, which by 1930 had finally won its war with Rum Row. But determined smugglers schemed ways to get through as demand for their product remained steady enough to inspire their creativity.

According to Bill McCoy, rumrunners outwitted authorities operating what he called "fresh fish boats." These were wide-hulled, fast vessels with special adaptations to the holds, including several below-deck storage compartments with trapdoors at the bottom of each compartment.

When pursued, the pilot pulled a lever. A trapdoor opened, and that compartment's load went to the bottom of the sea. Lightened, the smuggler gained speed while retaining a portion of his merchandise. If need be, the fleeing smuggler could empty his vessel compartment by compartment until, if finally caught, his captors found an empty boat.

In early summer, a fishing boat was seized by the Coast Guard at Ocean City's 9th Street Bridge. Abandoned by the crew, the deck was covered with a catch of fish. One of the holds below was empty, but hidden beneath its false bottom was a second hold, where searchers found $50,000 worth of liquor.

Sounds like the Coast Guard caught up again.

***

In April, Wildwood Police Chief Cobb, County Detective Umfreed and several officers were tried for illegal trespass. Their hearing was held in North Wildwood. They were accused of forcible entry and robbery by Wildwood property owner Albert Ward, whose place they'd raided earlier that month. Police had charged Ward with using his house as a distillery and showroom, making and selling booze. Ward was out on bail, awaiting his own trial.

Authorities seized four fifty-gallon stills, three hundred barrels of mash and twenty-five gallons of ready moonshine. A boisterous crowd jammed North Wildwood's courtroom to jeer at the plaintiff as Ward's complaint was quickly disposed of and the officers acquitted. The issue centered on whether Ward's house should have been treated as a private residence or illegal factory.

Prosecutor Millet Hand indicated he opposed Volstead raids upon private dwellings. "Whether or not this was a private dwelling house is another question." When Wildwood City attorney Harry Tenenbaum requested acquittal for the charged officers, Hand did not oppose the motion. The matter was put to rest, and the cops resumed their duties.

Meanwhile, the feds employed a new wrinkle to improve their effectiveness. Converging upon the county in early summer, they collected samples of beer and other drinks sold at area establishments to run chemical analyses to determine alcohol contents. New Jersey's latest top dry officer John Pennington planned nothing "new and spectacular" for enforcing the law, while the federal government shuffled bureaucracies, moving Prohibition from Treasury to Justice.

Pennington believed the most effective way to implement the law was to establish a "cooperative atmosphere between public officials and proprietors of places of pubic entertainment." A hopeful *Gazette* headlined its July 4 edition, "Liquor Laws to Be Quietly Enforced Here."

Cape May County welcomed what it hoped would be a busy summer season.

Cape May Harbor.
George F. Boyer
Historical Museum.

***

The oldest seashore resort in America, known as Cape Island until 1848, Cape May has welcomed tourists since colonial times. The town became a jewel of Victorian-era architecture by accident. In 1878, a massive fire destroyed entire blocks. The devastated area was rebuilt in the style of that era. An image was born of a place, staid and dignified, antithesis to loud and garish Wildwood to the immediate north.

But Cape May had its underside.

Authorities described it as a hangout for "notorious characters." Located by Schellenger's Landing, Cape May's fishing hub, the Sea View Inn was ideally situated near Cold Spring Inlet to accommodate day fishermen or those angling for pleasures of the evening.

The inn had experienced previous raids, so regulars knew the drill when agents visited in late July. The bar was hopping. Bartenders served drinks. Gamblers played slot machines. Women of easy virtue consorted. Locals and tourists mingled convivially until badges flashed and everyone raced for exits. Raiders let them go.

Officers arrested owner Jack Lilly, Lilly's son James and bartender Russell Hammer. They seized whisky by the pint and by the gallon.

Prior to the Civil War, the resort was known as a gambler's mecca, particularly appealing to southern gentlemen who wagered large sums while sampling choice champagnes during extended family vacations.

Hotel Macomber, Cape May, on fire. *Kathy Bresan*.

The Hotel Macomber featured a full basement, a catacomb of eight rooms. Gangsters allegedly used it for meetings during Prohibition, establishing a gambling den and fully stocked speakeasy where many private parties transpired.

The Queen's Hotel was originally built with an apothecary shop on the ground floor. Badly damaged in that 1878 fire, it too housed a speakeasy, with a brothel on the third floor.

Cape May was perhaps a sullied Queen of Resorts, but for those dedicated to enforcing dry laws, Wildwood would always be King Wet. The year 1930 proved no exception.

They knew where to go to find it, too. On the west side, police arrested William Pierce, who was operating a disorderly house. Finding assorted liquor on premises added a possession charge. Pierce and his wife were arrested. More raiders, under the direction of the ubiquitous Umfreed, hit the Little Night Club at Anglesea. They arrested Margaret Stanton for operating a disorderly house.

According to the *Leader*, authorities "swooped down on the place," finding barrels of beer, a slot machine and a roomful of revelers, all taken into police custody. Stanton posted bail, while partiers ponied up five dollars each.

The law hit the Biltmore Hotel at Cedar and Atlantic Avenues, nabbing proprietor David Ostreicher. The Biltmore provided a big yield, twenty-two halves of beer and two slot machines.

Chief Cobb led his war party around the corner to dependable Hamlet Hotel, where they arrested Mary Radwell and fetched another nineteen barrels of beer, along with bottles of whisky and two more slot machines.

The feds, who'd left the field to local authorities, flew into action, raiding the Pacific Hotel and arresting Jonathan James. The raiders were led by William Marshall, chief Prohibition agent from Atlantic City. They confiscated five barrels of beer and bottles of whisky. The politically connected James was brought before the U.S. commissioner in Atlantic City. He was eventually released on $1,000 bail.

Why the feds' interest in James? He was locally prominent. And he'd beaten the feds at the game previously. Maybe it was retribution. Maybe they figured local authorities wouldn't touch James. While the feds focused on James, local law continued cleaning up the rest of Wildwood. They hit a Poplar Avenue bungalow behind a boardwalk refreshment stand, seizing thirty-one cases of home brew and ninety gallons of mash.

They arrested Michael Earley and his sister, Margaret McLaughlin. Judge Way fined the guilty pair $475 upon the condition they leave Wildwood.

No one was leaving the Rio Grande Inn after Cobb and company paid a call in mid-August. Officers arrested thirteen people, seized liquor and impounded a slot machine. Harry "Curley" Sawyer, proprietor, was held on $2,000 bail for assorted violations. Nine men were fined $10 apiece for being "frequenters." Three women were fined $15 each for being "innmates" of the place.

Not a spelling error.

Sawyer's bail was furnished by Jonathan James.

It's worth noting the increased frequency of prostitution and gambling charges along with Volstead violations as the Prohibition era continued. Perhaps this trend evidences the growing influence of organized crime into other areas of vice. Or had society as a whole changed, resulting in greater desire for and acceptance of illicit activities that became regular menu items at speakeasies?

Jazz music, wild dancing, flappers, speakeasies and gambling. To some observers, all pointed to the moral downfall of America. The excitement of doing something illegal like drinking attracted people who never drank previously and would never frequent the Otten's Harbor section of Wildwood.

Hotel Grenoble, Wildwood, New Jersey. *George F. Boyer Historical Museum.*

Hotel Biltmore, a regular stop. *George F. Boyer Historical Museum.*

Drinking became fashionable. Middle-class regular folks drank. College kids binged. Women imbibed, titillated more perhaps by the prospect of being an "outlaw" than from contents of the glass. The era also introduced the cocktail. Mixing fruit juices, soda and whatever else was available not only enabled entrepreneurs to offer specialty drinks but also disguised the awful taste of bootleg booze.

How about the thrill of drinking in a speakeasy in Wildwood when the cops staged a raid?

Wildwood's finest provided opportunities, raiding the Little Club (Adam Kosobucki, proprietor), Surf Club (George O'Brien), Kelly's Café (George Kelly) and Elmira Hotel (Richard Grownley). Twenty barrels of beer, fifteen gallons of alcohol and twenty pints of whisky were confiscated. A second raid at Hotel Grenoble added twenty-one barrels of beer.

The trial of Grenoble proprietor Nick Rosolowitz further illustrated Hand's idea about how far the dry law should be enforced. Rosolowitz was not present during the Grenoble raid. His attorney, Harry Tenenbaum, warned jurors they'd better "flee from your homes, no longer your castles, when the law can snoop around at any time."

"Your home is still your castle," Hand countered. "What we raided was a barroom, not a home."

The jury found Rosolowitz guilty.

David Ostreicher of the Biltmore was acquitted of having twenty-four barrels of beer. A chemist's test showed the beer within the allowed alcohol content level.

William Marshall next led his federal agents to North Wildwood, where they struck the Anglesea Fishing Club and Anglesea Inn, arresting Andy Applegates, father and son. The booze count for the feds? Two dozen barrels of beer.

Some say lightning never strikes the same place twice. Law enforcement in Cape May County certainly did. In late summer 1930, Cobb and Umfreed returned to the Rio Grande Inn on a Sunday at 1:00 a.m. Curly Sawyer was arrested again for maintaining a disorderly house. His original $1,500 bail was upped by $2,000. Two waitresses from Penn's Grove were also arrested for a second time. Two other women were arrested as "innmates." Eight patrons were fined $10 each. A quantity of beer was seized, obviously fresh, since Curly had been cleaned out during the previous week's raid.

Then Cosmo Cappachione took center stage. In midsummer, Cappachione was charged with threatening to kill, larceny of an automobile, robbery, conspiracy, assault and concealing a crime. He and two accomplices allegedly seized a truck at gunpoint. The truck, owned by Pete Pittale of Hammonton, contained a shipment of liquor. It was empty when authorities found it. The truck was released to Richard Coney, who posted $2,000 bond.

The indictment against Cappachione stated he originally held up William Hickey at gunpoint, demanding $500. He threatened bodily harm to Hickey, Pittale and Coney if the money wasn't forthcoming.

When the trio didn't deliver, Cappachione took the truck.

Cappachione pleaded guilty to the larceny charges and was sentenced to three months in jail. An additional year sentence was suspended by Way. No action was taken on the other charges. Cappachione's case faded from the public eye after state police uncovered "the largest beer distribution operation yet found in the county."

Investigating complaints from Erma residents about men unloading truckloads of liquor, authorities arrived at a farmhouse to find four men removing 110 thirty-five-gallon kegs of beer from a five-ton Brockway truck. The men were arrested under bail totaling $10,000. Bail for one man, Ed Myers of Wildwood, was paid by Lewis Bishop. The others were bailed out by American Surety Company of New York.

A search of the farmhouse turned up ninety more kegs. Lester and Lois Riley, residing at the farmhouse, were arrested for possession. Their bail was paid by Jonathan James. The farm served as a drop or distribution point where trucks deposited illegal loads while removing empty barrels. The beer was found in the cement-lined cellar of the two-story farmhouse. The cellar contained two compartments with windows for ventilation and drop doors through which booze was conveyed.

The seized truck was specially designed to haul heavy weight. Kegs neatly piled three high and five across. The truck was equipped with dual tires in the rear and special springs capable of bearing ten-ton loads.

Myers was subsequently fined $500 for his role in the incident. "At least it's only beer," he offered in defense "Not hard liquor."

The *Gazette* reported another big capture at West Creek. State police arrested two men loading a Mack truck with two hundred cases of whisky. Along with the truck, officers captured a convoy car, bringing more booze from the landing. The driver stalled the car in the mud. In the commotion of working it free, no one heard the approaching footsteps of the law. Suspects escaped into the woods, but officials confiscated vehicles and cargoes.

In nearby Woodbine, Sheriff Rich arrested Moe Goodnard and Morris Lachow and seized $4,000 in assorted raw alcohol, empty bottles and fifty-gallon barrels. Authorities also found paraphernalia used to make bad booze

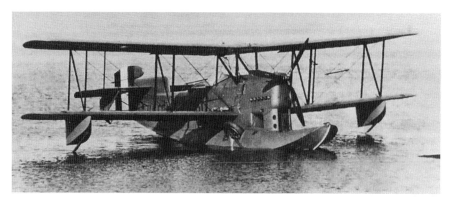

Hydroplane used to scout for rum schooners. *www.atlanticarea.uscg.*

appear to be good booze. These materials included brand-name labels, boxes, bottles and a sweating plant employed to extract whisky from old barrels. Two truckloads of evidence were hauled to Cape May Court House and stored in the county liquor "vault."

A far cry from the days of quibbling over paying watchmen to guard booze stacked in a cellar.

In another story, the *Gazette* declared Cape May the "busiest Coast Guard base on the east coast." The local station lived up to that superlative, capturing British schooner *Popocatepetl*, along with $200,000 worth of liquor, twenty crewmen prisoners and three contact boats.

The successful operation was planned by Lieutenant R.L. Burke, in charge at Cape May air base, working with pilot Ensign Jeff Ridgeway, who sighted the schooner. Burke coordinated air and sea efforts involved in the capture. The schooner initially attempted to escape but surrendered when shots were fired across its bow. *Popocatepetl* was towed to Philadelphia, where its cargo was unloaded by customs agents.

With winter descending upon the county, the usually quiet bayside hamlet of Pierce's Point made the news. Scotty was raided again.

Scott Errickson, who'd successfully defended himself against charges of Volstead violations, figured he'd try again. This time, he was arrested with nineteen others when raiders arrived at his property to find a party going full blast. Men tossing dice. Gamblers cranking slot machine handles. The bar crowded three deep, clearly open for business.

Raiders seized quarts of gin and whisky. Scotty was charged with keeping a disorderly house and held on $1,000 bail. His guests each paid $5 to get out of jail.

Roxanna Gandy, teacher and WCTU temperance educator. *Dennis Township Museum.*

Besting Prosecutor William Campbell his first go, this time Errickson tested his skills against Millet Hand. He didn't fare as well, drawing a fine for his losing effort.

***

The WCTU still insisted education and enforcement would solve the alcohol problem.

Meeting in Sea Isle City, the county chapter pushed for increased scientific temperance education in public schools while petitioning Judge Way to impose "heaviest possible sentences" on violators who failed to learn their lessons. Speakers pushed for greater WCTU involvement, urging members to attend court sessions, serve on grand juries and elect dry candidates for office.

The WCTU likely wasn't pleased with Federal Judge William Clark, who, in mid-December, declared the Eighteenth Amendment "invalid." Wets and dries agreed that Clark's word wouldn't be the last, anticipating action by the U.S. Supreme Court.

Clark's ruling revolved around interpreting the method of approving the Eighteenth Amendment. The U.S. Constitution, he argued, in Article Five, states there are two ways to amend: two-thirds vote of state legislatures or calling a constitutional convention. Clark contended that in transferring power from state to federal government, the latter method became more appropriate.

However, as suggested by Lanning Myers, editor of the *Wildwood Journal Tribune*, "it isn't likely the Supreme Court will invalidate the 18th at this point in its history." The only way to do that would be to replace it with another amendment.

Clark may have stirred the pot, but the long-awaited report of the Wickersham Commission brought it to a boil. Avoiding discussion of the merits of the Prohibition law, commission members offered a range of opinions, ignoring the biggest problem as matters stood in 1930: Prohibition lacked public support needed to enforce it.

As 1930 drew to a close, dry advocates wanted stricter enforcement and more education while wets tested law enforcement capabilities in their efforts to get what they wanted. Namely, liquid refreshment—like that seized by the Coast Guard on New Year's Eve.

After an exciting chase, the *Lily of the Valley* was captured along with five hundred sacks of holiday cheer worth fifty dollars a bag. Would more lilies bloom in the Atlantic in 1931?

1931

It started like the previous year ended…with raids. According to the *New York Times*, federal agents seized thousands of dollars' worth of liquor while arresting thirty.

At 6:00 p.m. on the dot, agents hit twenty-two places simultaneously, under orders from Deputy Prohibition Administrator Louis Tutt, orchestrating from Newark. The raid was led by Chief Agent William Marshall commanding fifty-eight agents. Armed with warrants, they maneuvered like pieces of precision clockwork, locating, sampling and destroying supplies of beer and wine. Copper coils of stills were twisted beyond recognition and rendered useless.

Nightclubs, hotels, speakeasies in Wildwood, Anglesea and Cape May were raided. Another claim of "largest raid in the history of Cape May County," this one might actually have been correct.

Many of the establishments visited had been raided during the last "largest clean-up" and the one before that. This time felt different. Calm persisted among authorities going about their business. Owners and bartenders were herded into custody at Wildwood City Hall without much theatrics. Bails were fixed at $1,000 per arrestee. Justice of the Peace Lanning Myers, present by prearrangement, expedited proceedings.

According to Prohibition officials, the raids had been planned for weeks, "set up" a few nights before when undercover buyers made purchases of illegal liquor, securing required "cause" evidence at each place marked for action. Agents from Camden and Philly and D.C. participated, without consulting or warning local authorities, who seemed as stunned by the raids as those targeted.

Many of the names were familiar to those following the local booze brawl over the years. The establishments raided and their proprietors comprised a who's who of Volstead violators: Brass Rail (Joe Russo), Louie's (Lou Compare), Dominick Cappachione, Bradley Café (Herb Mackin), Club Café (Joe Zech), Central Inn (Michael Donnelly), Kelly's Café (Ed Meehan), Grenoble Hotel (Mike Wyshwanik), Biltmore Hotel (David Ostreicher), Penn-Wood Hotel (Hugh McCardell), Victor Café (Rocco Turchi), Hamlet Hotel (John McGowan), Henie Hotel (May Henie), Little Club Café (Dominick Piro), Tip Toe Café (Joe Piro), Little Night Club (Margaret Stanton), Ocean View Fish Market (John Press), Royal Hotel (Adam Kosobucki), Walnut House (Martin Hogensang), Billy's Café (William Deaver), Sea-View Inn (Harry Redding) and Erico's Grocery (Erico Pultripelli).

Before the dazed looks faded, establishments were padlocked by order of U.S. District Court in Trenton. The Coast Guard followed up, capturing a rumrunner at rest on a sand bar near Corson's Inlet while it rendezvoused with courier boats. Caught in the act, smugglers attempted to jettison the goods, but officials salvaged most of the haul.

Hands Mill beside "major highway" into the county. *George F. Boyer Historical Museum.*

A total of 125 cases were seized.

More turned up later. Cases of whisky, valued at $60–$100 each, and barrels of malt worth $400 washed ashore. News of what the incoming tide carried brought swarms of "volunteers" to the beach to help authorities salvage what washed ashore.

Hereford Inlet station also staged a successful raid, seizing over four hundred cases of booze on a lonely road near Dennis Creek. Total value of this haul, which included three captured vehicles, was $35,000. Each truck carried two hundred cases of Canadian whisky. The booze had been transported up the creek by boat during the night. The plan was to conceal the liquor under farm produce being shipped to Philadelphia.

Dennis Creek was a major port and shipbuilding center in the nineteenth century. Schooners were built and launched there, making it a significant commercial hub for the county. At one time, more than fifty ship captains lived in nearby Dennisville.

Its glory days largely passed by the 1930s, Dennis Creek still offered an ideal means of transporting illegal cargoes to isolated spots among marshes near the main highway crossing the creek between today's towns of Dennisville and South Dennis.

***

Authorities appeared everywhere in 1931, sniffing for booze but finding small amounts. A drip here, a few drops there, no hidden caches or secret drops. In early June, county detectives descended upon Stone Harbor, raiding three spots around the 96th Street Harbor area.

At Shelter Haven, they arrested owner Leo Kenner, confiscating two half barrels of beer. At Bungalow Tea Room, Babe Latour and Arthur Lang were nabbed along with two more barrels of brew. The Locust Inn gave up three halves along with seven quarts of whisky and Ed Powers. The owners were released on $1,000 bail apiece. Small change compared to Wildwood but a day's excitement in sleepy Stone Harbor.

Ocean City cops raided eight places one night. They arrested seven people. The biggest catch was Walt Scull, a former bank clerk who operated a parking lot in the center of town. He was arrested on the lot, carrying twelve pints of whisky. That's how it went in early summer 1931. Smaller raiding parties obtained modest results.

Woodbine didn't produce much either. Garage operator Alex May's second-floor apartment housed a small "adulterating" business. A few

Schooners anchored at Dennis Creek. *Dennis Township Museum.*

Dennis Creek looking south to Delaware Bay. *Dennis Township Museum.*

five-gallon cans of "supposed" alcohol, empty bottles labeled "Old Overholt" and "Johnny Walker Scotch," coloring agents, funnels, a hand mixer, a glue gun. No still or armed gangs or modified trucks, just a one-man operation.

Even dependable Wildwood was subdued. Umfreed and Cobb hit the hamlet again. They seized a few barrels of beer and a slot machine and arrested Mary Radwell. She paid her fine and went her way. The county needed some excitement.

Then the Cuban Revolution arrived.

Guns and ammunition and nine desperadoes were hauled into Wildwood City Hall in handcuffs.

Alarmists claimed they were bank robbers. Highwaymen waylaying motorists. Gun-toting gangsters strong-arming businesses. They were even accused of holding up a dance marathon—robbed the dancers, too.

None of it was true. The truth was much stranger.

The nine belonged to a contingent of one hundred revolutionaries out of Atlantic City trying to reach Cuba. Unable to connect with their larger vessel heading south, they steered their small vessel into Cold Spring Inlet. The men went ashore for supplies. The Coast Guard stopped the boat from returning to sea, stranding the men in the county. Some tried leaving by train. They were arrested. Others hailed taxis to drive to Atlantic City. They were detained.

After they finally managed to tell their story, they were released. Without their weapons. But Wildwood enjoyed the brief non-Volstead excitement. The Cuban Revolution simmered for another era.

***

State police found it on a farm near Belleplain. A still, but not just a still. Authorities believed they'd uncovered the device used by a bootlegger gang producing alcohol on a "wholesale scale."

Typical hyperbole described the still as "gigantic." The operation was "huge."

Detective Umfreed initially led raiders to a Woodbine garage where they arrested five men and confiscated a truck containing 122 five-gallon cans of alcohol. The truck was fitted out with a false bottom and side panels for concealing liquor. Following up on tips they'd received, authorities swooped down on the farm, where they found the fully operating manufacturing facility. Estimated value of the equipment alone was over $25,000.

Proud raiders pose in front of prize in woods near Woodbine. *Dennis Township Museum.*

The still was described as a "column type." Steamed water pumped through the device quickened the distillation process. Set up in an old chicken house, the still was cooking when officers arrived. A 250-gallon tank on the roof contained mash. The tank was pipe-connected to the still, steadily feeding mash to the cooker at a rate of 50 gallons per hour. Raiders found 250 barrels of mash awaiting transformation into liquid gold. Eight tons of brown sugar and 300 pounds of brewer's yeast were also confiscated. The farm was owned by Dick Chiapelli, operator of a store in Belleplain. He was arrested along with Jack Elberg, owner of the garage.

The Coast Guard matched Umfreed's "big score" in Belleplain when it captured the *Allegro*. *Allegro* was taken in midsummer, sixty miles at sea off Cape May. The 125-foot pleasure yacht sat "low in the water" according to the boatswain who first spotted it.

"Like she was heavily loaded."

Authorities ordered *Allegro* to halt, firing a round when the yacht failed to respond. A three-hour chase ensued, covering more than thirty miles out to sea before *Allegro* surrendered, unable to run any more. Raiders found booze worth $120,000. They arrested twelve men.

But where were the women?

Initial reports described two women, depicted as "society girl passengers," aboard Allegro. Subsequent rumors claimed they were wives of two crew members. Passengers, wives, it didn't matter. The crew denied having women aboard, and there were no signs of female presence when the arrestees were shipped to Camden for incarceration.

The *Gazette* eventually shed some light on that mystery. The crew had been disguised as "yachtsmen," and women were seen aboard as a "distraction" from *Allegro's* true purpose. The yacht left New York with the girls, picked up a shipment of liquor from a large steamer anchored off Atlantic City. They planned to dispose of the liquor in Atlantic City and docked there for about two weeks, waiting for a chance to act. The girls were noticed there, comporting themselves like "rich yacht people." Finally, the crew suspected they were being closely watched and took to sea.

The confiscated liquor consisted of two thousand cases, valued at $60 per case. It was brought to Philadelphia aboard the cutter *Pulaski*. The crew, all from Brooklyn, were eventually released on combined $35,000 bail, bond provided by Lexington Surety. Their attorney immediately complained the yacht was taken outside U.S. territorial waters. "We'll come to that later," overruled Commissioner Wynn Armstrong, who conducted the hearing.

The hearing did produce one tantalizing tidbit. According to the *Gazette*, the crew provided information promising to lead to a "big breakthrough" in authorities' battle against organized liquor trafficking. The yacht, valued at $375,000, was owned by Charles Robbins, address listed as "Pennsylvania Hotel." Robbins was an alleged member of a Philadelphia-based syndicate running liquor using boats like *Allegro*.

Allegro was finally captured because its three fuel tanks burned up during the chase. Once a brightly painted shiny gem, *Allegro's* battered hull made a sad sight as it had to be towed into Philly.

But whatever did become of those girls?

***

It wouldn't be summer in Wildwood without a raid on Hotel Elmira. This time, the arrested proprietor was Herb McMachin. It's interesting how often ownership changed in these establishments. Was it the nature of seasonal resort business or a response to added stresses of ownership during Prohibition? Didn't matter. McMachin was hauled in and his liquor seized.

Raiders also hit the Hotel Blackstone and arrested Tom Dauganais along with several patrons. He was fined $1,000. The patrons paid $7.50 each in fines. Price of floor show and two-drink minimum.

How much was the county feeling the effect of the Depression, and how much was the seeming quiet the result of law enforcement's effectiveness?

New Jersey beer drinkers had to be thirsty. Truckloads of foamy amber were seized on a regular basis. Seashore resorts dried up, turning the barrier islands into desert islands. There was home brew, but the quality coming out of kitchen setups lent bitter truth to Will Rogers's assessment of Prohibition: "It was better than no booze at all."

Barely.

As summer faded into mellow autumn, law enforcement savored recent successes. A statewide beer operation had been stopped colder than a frosted mug. An estimated $300,000 in beer and seventy trucks used to bring it to the parched masses were taken in raids.

The feds dispatched an additional 350 agents to New Jersey. Major highways were monitored, backroads closely watched. Railroad cars, once a reliable way to transport large cargoes, were scrutinized. With booze so hard to come by, public sentiment, the *Wildwood Leader* reported, "will be aroused to high pitch to repeal the 18th amendment when the Republicans hold their national convention" for the 1932 election.

In Cape May County, smugglers responded by switching to cars to move beer instead of trucks, settling for smaller loads that had better chances of making it through. Drops were set up for cars delivering a few barrels to resort customers. This was given high priority by smugglers since the shore resorts comprised a significant percentage of their business.

The *Leader* noted the cost of making a half barrel of beer was less than $1.50. That beer sold for $35.70. Significant indeed.

***

The *New York Times* reported on October 14 that a $5 million liquor ring, centered in the Delaware Valley area, had fallen. This massive organization generated $2 million annual sales through a coordinated effort using land and water transportation, modern communication technology and vast production and storage facilities. All laid low by a trap developed by federal authorities for over a year.

The ring operated at what legitimate businesses consider the wholesale level. No orders below case lots. Liquor was brought in by courier boats from supply ships anchored off New Jersey, landed at various drop points and loaded onto trucks. It was then delivered to local warehouses or cutting plants where, depending on the product, it was stored until called for or modified and rebottled. Ordered liquor was then shipped to smaller operators.

Raiders uncovered twelve outlaw radio stations, six rumrunning boats, two cutting plants, a massive warehouse in Delaware County, Pennsylvania, two other warehouses in New York and Atlantic City to service those specific areas and two "executive offices" in center city Philadelphia, one at 15th and Chestnut Streets, one block from city hall. The other office was located at the Bankers Trust Building at Juniper and Walnut. The ring's finances were coordinated through Franklin Mortgage Company as well. That entity was connected with well-known Philadelphia criminal elements.

Three dozen arrest warrants had already been executed when the *Times* article appeared. Another fifty were in the works. Arrests were ongoing. More significantly, the feds had acquired lists of names of those who'd done business with the ring, both vendors and customers. They also gathered over five hundred incriminating documents from the office.

And the government had learned the name of the ring's "operational head." J. Frank Hilton. The North Wildwood lad.

The *Philadelphia Inquirer* reported that shortly after the initial raids, one of the ring's "mother" ships, *Nan and Edna*, was seized by a Coast Guard destroyer along with a courier vessel, *Winnie Estelle*. The capture resulted from subterfuge. Authorities used the ring's secret code to broadcast over one of its captured radio stations, arranging a rendezvous where both vessels were intercepted by the destroyer. That success was sweetened by the additional capture of seven hundred cases of liquor.

Wiretapping, code breaking, spies, fake radio messaging—stuff of espionage thrillers—contributed to breaking the ring. A task force of agents recruited from outside the region required more than six months of secretive work.

Events happened quickly after the initial break. Within days, fugitives wanted in connection with the investigation conveyed messages to authorities through attorneys about surrendering. These messages were conveyed by Congressman Benjamin Goldin, also an attorney, whose clients included Max "Boo Boo" Hoff. Negotiations proceeded while investigators learned the ring was actually part of a larger organization of what the *Inquirer* termed "sharper-witted men," headquartered in Montreal.

Apparently, the growing Depression affected the ring's operations like any other business. Even as the workings of the local ring unraveled, business continued. Authorities learned the operation was currently experiencing a cash flow problem. Orders came in—demand wasn't slowing down—but customers often couldn't pay, and the ring's accounting department experienced difficulty reconciling the books.

That's how the feds learned of the Montreal connection. The main office had begun the process of doing what any large corporation would do in this situation. Cut its losses. The apparent goal was to "eliminate the Philadelphia division," the *Inquirer* reported. It didn't need much imagination to visualize methods it might use to accomplish this goal.

Meanwhile, the feds continued securing ring assets, including $40,000 in liquor stored at a warehouse in Upper Darby along with gallons of "stuff" found in an office in center city. Mastermind Hilton supervised quite a workforce as well: a sales division, with each salesman assigned a specific geographical area. Orders were submitted to the main office on Chestnut Street. Other departments handled cutting, order filling and shipping. Subdivisions directed the rum fleet; others handled trucking and communications.

The ring couriered money to Montreal to buy liquor at St. Pierre Island. Liquor was brought in from Canada or Europe. All shipments were bonded. Communications were handled in code. Rumrunners were provided current sets of Coast Guard and geologic survey sounding charts of the New Jersey coast with coordinates converted into the ring's code. Radio stations broadcast coded rendezvous dates, times, locations, facilitating smooth transfers of goods from supply ship to couriers.

Speedboats were typically used as couriers, but at one point, the operation had grown so large and brazen that larger towed barges were used to haul in the goods. On land, truck dispatchers arranged transportation to and from drop points and from there to distribution centers or directly to customers.

The ring's existence had been known to authorities for years, according to the *Inquirer*, but the feds bided their time. Gathering evidence. Learning its system. They tapped phones, recording extensive conversation, most of it routine-sounding business talk. They occasionally staged "show" raids using local law enforcement to encourage the false impression that no one was aware of the bigger picture. They also developed what the paper called a "very tender list" of 1,500 names of customers, including many prominent Philadelphia citizens

Hilton's role seemed to be that of problem solver, particularly involving the Jersey shore, where he was presumably expert. He was described by the *Inquirer* as the "mastermind of the operation," but the paper also referred to him as a "little fellow, measured against the big money backers of the ring" operating out of Montreal. Hilton was apparently in from the beginning, helping to set up operations, seeing that expenses were paid and both booze and cash flowed. He also made decisions on such details as how many radio stations to use and where to place them, as well as setting up shipments from Canada along with transport at each step in the transaction process. He established protection for key ring properties.

All of this was learned from review of hours of wiretapped conversations. "What if the men [agents] from Philly crash the radio station if they find out where it is?" Hilton was asked in one taped talk. "They try to get by the boys with the shotguns, look in the obit column tomorrow," he replied.

Guess he arranged that, too.

On one occasion he mentioned going down to Atlantic City "to get drunk and have a helluva good time." Not once in the recordings did he mention his hometown.

***

The Coast Guard enjoyed the last move of 1931's campaign against the "Hilton gang." After a six-month cat-and-mouse game, culminating in a final desperate race for the cover of secluded bayside coves, authorities caught the speedster rumrunner *Baboon* a few days before Christmas.

It was carrying lots of Christmas cheer, one thousand cases of liquor. No arrests were made, as the crew fled.

The *Baboon*'s long career had been aided by its coded communications via radio through the ring's network of radio stations. With that system broken, the Coast Guard finally made a monkey out of the *Baboon*.

Frank Hilton remained a wanted man, on the lam from authorities. The smuggling ring was in disarray. The Coast Guard maintained control over area waters, and local law enforcement's raids choked off overland supplies. As 1931 came to its end, the war on booze appeared to have deescalated into a mop-up operation against small-time operators working out in the woods.

Was Prohibition in southern New Jersey finally succeeding?

The long-anticipated Wickersham Report was a letdown for those hoping for a definitive strategy from the federal government. While the report opposed repeal of the Eighteenth Amendment, it also opposed state and local involvement in the liquor business or changes to the law to allow beer and wine.

Its solutions for the future? More money for enforcement. More vigorous prosecutions. Enforcement left solely to the federal government.

Hoover disagreed with the latter. He believed states should take the lead role. There was disagreement among commission members about those results. Some members favored repeal. Some called for modified Volstead.

The only consensus about the commission's effort was that it resolved nothing. The 1932 presidential election shaped up to be another wet versus dry, urban versus rural, immigrant versus native, Democrat versus Republican campaign, with the addition of one huge issue.

The Great Depression.

1932

"All Prohibition has accomplished with its holy crusade is to augment vastly the number of boozers in the US," H.L. Mencken wrote in 1932, "while converting the trade in alcohol once a lawful business into a criminal racket." As Prohibition entered its twelfth year, a growing number of Americans agreed with Mencken's assessment. *Literary Digest* conducted another poll of five million Americans in 1932; it revealed that 73 percent called for an end to the Great Experiment.

The AAPA, originally organized to push for modification of the Volstead Act to allow beer and light wines, was one of the loudest and best-funded voices calling for repeal. Freedom of choice, cost of enforcement, rise of organized crime were all factors AAPA used in its arguments. Money was possibly the biggest factor.

By 1932, a number of wealthy Americans became backers of AAPA, among them Pierre DuPont, originally a vocal dry. Wealthy businessmen reasoned that allowing alcohol would create a substantial source of revenue for the federal government as it had prior to 1920. Much of that lost revenue had been replaced by taxes on personal income, initiated by the Sixteenth Amendment, which men like DuPont considered an unfair and onerous burden. Their position? Repeal the Eighteenth Amendment and the Sixteenth could be repealed too.

In Trenton, the state assembly, controlled by a Democratic majority, approved a measure repealing the state's Prohibition enforcement law, the Hobart Act, as one of its first items of business to start the new year.

Legislators predicted that was just a beginning, arguing that genuine change would occur only when states' rights were given higher priority over federal power in administering Prohibition law until eventual national repeal.

Legislators lobbied Congress to amend Volstead to allow light wine and beer, the *Wildwood Tribune Journal* reported, noting the activity was a "sign that popular sentiment had moved away from the position of the Wickersham Commission," which advocated additional funding for enforcement. "We are a wet state," an unnamed Republican legislator summarized, "Let us be consistently wet so our congressmen know the people of New Jersey demand relief from the present intolerable conditions."

While state government worked toward reducing enforcement of the dry law, Cape May County prosecutor Millet Hand castigated local police for not doing enough to "end violations of prohibition and gambling laws." He hinted at employing out-of-county detectives to do the job, evoking unpleasant memories of the Guarantee Detectives, hired by his predecessor.

Hand also threatened to prosecute police officers "seemingly derelict in their duty." He specifically cited Wildwood, North Wildwood and Cape May as problem areas. Inland towns, the *Gazette* pointed out, were not included in Hand's criticism because law enforcement in those areas fell under jurisdiction of state police since, other than a small police department at Woodbine, there was no local law enforcement.

Coast Guard authorities shared Hand's concern about what the *Gazette* termed a "laxity of rum blockade." State Prohibition Director John Pennington charged Coast Guard crewmen, indeed entire crews, with allowing smugglers to freely operate on Delaware Bay.

Activity had increased bayside in recent years, with smugglers using smaller craft to access remote creeks along the marshy bay coast. A smart adjustment on their part, given the dominating Coast Guard presence in the Atlantic. The Coast Guard investigated itself. While Chief Inspector Captain William Wheeler didn't find wholesale corruption, he did suspend one man stationed at Base Nine in Cape May. Charges were also filed against an unspecified number of men.

While Coast Guard honesty was investigated, rumrunners landed a sizable cargo at West Creek in early March. They were caught by state police, working off a "mysterious tip." Two troopers arrived at the landing to find men unloading five hundred cases from a barge onto horse-drawn wagons that would convey the booze to trucks waiting near the highway. The bootleggers had learned from experience. A previous attempt to land booze at West Creek had been thwarted partly because the smugglers had brought their vehicles to the water, where one car became stuck in mud.

The Coast Guard did manage to catch tuna in early 1932. This was fish of a different kind. A rumrunner vessel named *Tuna* had broken down in Delaware Bay off Villas. Authorities seized the craft and cargo but not before the crew had swum to shore, escaping.

The *Tuna* floundered because of excess weight, three hundred cases of assorted liquors. The craft was suspected of being a courier for three mother ships operating just beyond twelve miles off Cape May. Those larger ships were rumored to carry twelve thousand cases each.

The Coast Guard managed to float the bloated *Tuna* to Cape May Harbor. That was the preliminary event. In late May, Coast Guard pulled of a $350,000 triple play that dispelled all doubt about its focus.

A tip to Base Nine facilitated capture of the collier *Maurice Tracey* docked in New York and the bullet-ridden rumrunner *Love Bird* at Gardiner's Basin in Atlantic City. State police working in cooperation completed the triple capture, seizing 250 cases of booze from an oyster schooner on the Maurice River.

The schooner *Bernardine Williams*, from the Chesapeake Bay area, was taken near Matt's Landing by troopers, surprising a landing party of fifteen men loading booze into trucks.

The collier in New York proved that coastal steamers had been used to collect huge amounts of liquor to transport to the East Coast. Rum Row might be gone, but there were still some major smugglers operating in the Atlantic. The *Tracey*, along with a second collier and two tankers, was spotted by air reconnaissance from Cape May and reported to customs authorities in New York. The Coast Guard added to the government haul, two rum schooners taken at Delaware Bay breakwater.

Assigned to search for what the *Leader* called "the phantom ship thought to harbor kidnappers of the Lindbergh baby," cutters from Cape May instead snagged two vessels carrying a combined value of $100,000 in choice liquors. The smugglers were running without lights when the *Hermes* ordered them to halt, firing warning shots when it instead picked up speed. *Hermes*'s pursuit was joined by the cutter *Tiger*.

The Coast Guard arrested five men, held on $5,000 bail each. Their cargo was stored at the Philadelphia Customs House. The capture of the *Bernardine Williams* tied in with the Hilton ring, suggested a *Baltimore Sun* story about smuggling charges out of Maryland. Eastern Shore oyster boats were used to smuggle liquor into Chesapeake and Delaware Bay.

Listed among thirty-seven conspirators indicted in that area's ring were a few New Jerseyans, including Frank Hilton. The *Sun* listed his alias in Baltimore as A.M. Grant. The article also indicated that headquarters for this particular ring was in either Bivalve, a small fishing port on the bay in Cumberland County, or Wildwood.

Indictments against the Philadelphia ring were issued in May. A dozen lawyers appeared in court. Their pleas for release were rejected. The 35-page federal indictment listed 66 names with 50 indicted under 139 separate counts. The ring had become a noose.

Topping the lists in both Philly and Baltimore was the man the *Inquirer* designated "the big shot"—Frank Hilton. As of May 21, Hilton remained a fugitive from justice.

***

Meanwhile, local small fry struggled along on the drops of booze they managed to slip past local law enforcement.

Wholesome-named Dad's Place in Tuckahoe was raided, owners Walter Huby and Howard Fredericks arrested.

Raiders found a small brewing operation. A gross of bottles of home brew, two fermenting crocks, eight cans of malt, one hundred pounds of cane sugar, quantities of caps and cappers. Today, that's a nanobrewery.

In addition, a five-gallon still was found in Fredericks's barn, next to Dad's. Raiders confiscated mash and one hundred pounds of corn.

County detectives traveled south to the original whaling area of Town Bank to raid another home brewery. Harry Stoudt was throwing a shindig at his George's Café when the law arrived. Two dozen dancers froze in midstep. Beer stopped flowing. The party was over, except for raiders helping themselves to 582 bottles of home brew. They also took away fixings for the next batch, malt, caps and a capping machine. Harry was arrested, and the band packed off without playing an encore.

Beer consumption initially declined with Prohibition. Big breweries closed. Bootleggers didn't waste valuable cargo space on cases or kegs of beer when hard stuff paid much more. Beer also tended to have a shorter shelf life. Plus, it was actually cheaper to produce adulterated hard liquor.

Nevertheless, home brewers created a significant industry for raw materials. U.S. corn sugar production rose 500 percent after 1919 from 157 million to 900 million pounds a year. Corn sugar is essential for home brewing.

Curly Sawyer wouldn't have to worry about any more raids on his Rio Grande Inn. A mid-May fire destroyed the inn, eulogized by the *Leader* as one of Wildwood's "pre-Prohibition havens for fishermen." Sawyer owned the inn for three years, during which time it was subjected to frequent attention from authorities. Sawyer gamely fought the blaze with a garden hose while firefighters from across the island fought the blaze but to no avail.

May was a rough month for Wildwood cops as well. City commissioners reduced salaries up to 40 percent for the entire department and demoted senior officers. Longtime chief Oakford Cobb was demoted to patrolman, as was Captain Lynn Forcum, another face familiar to Volstead violators. Mike Sheehan was promoted to acting police chief.

Newly elected commissioner K.K. Kirby initiated wholesale changes in the entire city workforce, but police were especially hit. Kirby's name had frequently appeared in Prohibition news stories, usually related to his ownership of an express trucking company. Sheehan was the patrolman involved in an altercation with federal officers who subsequently charged him with interfering with their raid on a local speakeasy.

To some, Kirby's actions were punitive, retaliating for Cobb's role in leading raids to enforce Volstead. Cobb was still technically chief during appeal of his demotion to the state supreme court. Acting chief Sheehan assigned him to work the switchboard.

***

Wildwood police might have been in disarray, but the feds continued raiding as the summer season got started. They hit Hotel Elmira before crossing East Schellenger Avenue to Hotel Lyndhurst. Small quantities of liquor were secured at each stop. Word spread of their presence. A crowd gathered to watch and follow agents as they crossed Wildwood to the Philadelphia House. There, they seized another small quantity of beer.

Meanwhile, state and county authorities worked the west side with limited success. A few arrests were made at the Poplar Cafe. A few bottles of booze were confiscated. They raided Club Café, which had recently reopened for the summer after being padlocked for prior infractions. Owner Adam Kosobucki was an unlucky fellow. Arrested again, more of his liquor seized. This time, agents also seized a slot machine, adding its possession to their charges.

Wildwood's reorganized finest, under orders from Sheehan to "clean up the town," joined the festivities near Otten's Harbor, raiding the Royal

Gardens and the Love Nest, Big Mose Caldwell's place, seizing home brew at each location.

They also arrested Spencer Burke of Dock Street. Burke was of special interest to authorities for another reason. As Burke was local conduit for the late Mickey Duffy's narcotics smuggling operation, his arrest was particularly significant for authorities.

With the law snooping everywhere, the beer supply dried up, and with the summer season in full swing, Wildwood speak operators were hard-pressed to find beverages to slake tourist thirsts. Conditions parched further when authorities raided a wildcat brewery in Belleplain. The operation had been set up in chicken housing on a farm leased by a group of Newark men who flew the coop, avoiding arrest. Raiders confiscated two five-hundred-gallon wooden vats, four steel tanks, thirty-two empty barrels and several barrels of finished beer.

County Detective Umfreed encored, finding a massive still in Ocean View. Actually, two stills, 500 and 1,500 gallons, respectively.

The steam gauge read a sultry 195 degrees when raiders, following another "mysterious tip," arrived at a recently constructed three-story frame building on property of Rosario Ciaurelli. The building had been leased by men from "north Jersey." Coils on the still rose thirty feet. The device itself stood so high a tower had been added to the main structure to house its uppermost extremities. Underground vats were installed to store alcohol.

In addition to the still, authorities seized five-gallon cans of alcohol, twelve-gallon cans of molasses, electric motors, hand pumps, hundred-gallon sheet metal containers, bags of coal, quantities of copper tubing and other supplies. The alcohol was destroyed and the entire works dismantled for storage at the county building.

Booze somehow still appeared in local establishments. The "laws" kept making it disappear.

The August 11 *Leader* reported that authorities continued their "relentless campaign to rid the county of gambling houses and speakeasies." Spurred on by Prosecutor Hand, they raided a number of areas, starting in Wildwood.

Spencer Burke was raided again. He was arrested again. His liquor was taken again.

Burke would eventually go to jail, not for booze, but for his role in narcotics smuggling. On one of the raids of his place, agents found $20,000 worth of uncut drugs. To get an idea of the street value of that, cocaine cost $4 per ounce for the seller. Buyers paid between $60–$130 per ounce.

Narcotics were smuggled into Wildwood to Burke's "finishing factory" on Otten's Harbor. His factory was also raided, and thousands of dollars in supplies used to cut dope were confiscated, along with quantities of street-ready cocaine, heroin, morphine and opium.

Raiders also revisited Schellenger Avenue and the Imperial Café, arresting owner Charles Raucci. Beer was seized. Same thing happened at Applegate's. Andrew incarcerated, beer confiscated. John Keenan's café near the boardwalk yielded more beer and another unlucky entrepreneur.

The Little Ritz offered some variety: eighty-five pint bottles of rot gut whisky. Clearly, the quality of merchandise had deteriorated since Rum Row. Cosmos Cappachione of Little Ritz provided the biggest haul, slot machines and whisky. He was held on $2,000 bail.

County and state law revisited Dock Street. Carl Linquist had hidden his beer under the floor. They sniffed it out. Neighbor Mary Pearson concealed home brew in her attic. They ferreted that out. Robert Fawcett was caught transporting eight barrels of beer somehow squeezed into his car. They rolled them out.

Summer ended on a decidedly dry note.

***

Defying the Coast Guard's tight watch over area waters, diehard rumrunners geared up for another round. An unnamed "federal authority" told the *New York Times* that five regional liquor gangs "had pooled resources to clean up" before the end of the year. They'd invested over $1 million to bring seven mother ships along with a flotilla of speedy couriers to waters off southern New Jersey, outside the twelve-mile limit.

Coast Guard seaplanes spotted the fleet loading cases of booze onto couriers. Speedier launches were dispatched to cut them off before they landed their cargoes. Meanwhile, destroyers drew a tight net around the fleet.

One rumrunner was captured; another was grounded and destroyed by fire near the entrance of Delaware Bay.

The smugglers tried evading capture, dropping a thick smoke screen. The ruse enabled two ships to escape. The sixty-foot *Celerity* surrendered. It carried seven hundred cases of liquor. The sixty-foot *Appomattox*, carrying six hundred cases, was destroyed, bursting into flames as its crew leaped to safety. Coast Guard gunfire had ignited the blaze.

Before it was over, more than seventy ships had joined the rum invasion between New England and Cape May. The Coast Guard responded in force, five destroyers and nine 125-foot offshore patrol boats joining the already formidable dry fleet.

The *Baltimore Sun* reported that federal officials believed the large concentration this time suggested that rumrunners sensed their days were numbered—not because of the success of law enforcement but because they believed Prohibition was about to end and they wanted to make one last big score.

In November 1932, Americans elected a new president. Franklin Roosevelt's victory marked the end of an era. Twelve years of Republican-led government and Republican socioeconomic policymaking. People craved change, dramatic change that would pull the country out of the Depression.

They demanded change in Prohibition law as well. "We want beer!" placards waved at the Democratic convention and anti-Volstead rallies nationwide. FDR would give it to them.

***

In Philadelphia, justice slowly moved forward in its prosecution of the "Hilton Rum Ring." At the end of December, thirty-three of fifty leaders of the $5 million operation refused to plead to indictments charging them with conspiracy to violate Prohibition and customs laws. A trial date was set for February 6, 1933.

Bench warrants were issued for fugitives, including Frank Hilton, whom the *Inquirer* persisted in calling the "key man and mastermind." Hilton had eluded agents when they raided his office at Chestnut Street in October. As 1932 ended, he remained missing.

1933

In 1933, after more than thirteen dry years and with economic depression digging deep into America's psyche, a new president legalized beer as one of his first steps in leading the nation's recovery.

Nine days after FDR's inauguration, Congress amended the Volstead Act to allow 3.2 percent beer.

Critics asserted that Volstead failed because it underestimated the ingenuity of lawbreakers' efforts to circumvent the law. It underestimated their ability to subvert those whose task was to enforce that law. Mostly, drys missed the mark in assuming people would obey the law even though they didn't like it, simply because it was the law.

But for all that, Prohibition was far from over.

***

The *Wildwood Leader* interviewed the oldest living woman in Cape May County on her ninetieth birthday. Hannah Ludlam Townsend of Dennisville lived her entire life at her family's ancestral home. Her father, prominent Quaker William Smith Townsend, was a landowner whose holdings included present-day Woodbine and Belleplain. Active in Whig Party politics, he once hosted presidential hopeful Henry Clay.

Miss Hannah was four years old when Clay stayed at Five Chimneys. Her Townsend, Smith and Ludlam roots went back to the very beginnings of the county. What were her feelings about Prohibition?

"Liquor once saved my life, when I was dying of pneumonia," she told the *Leader*. Even so, she opposed repeal. "Liquor is too much of a temptation to young people. I am in favor of having the amendment enforced."

The *Julia Davis* was the Coast Guard's first catch of 1933. The seventy-foot schooner was seized at dock in Cape May after a spirited chase. Beneath a load of fish, authorities found fifty cases of concealed liquor.

But authorities made their biggest catch in Canada. Frank Hilton was captured by Montreal police. Arrested and held without bail, Hilton awaited a hearing on extradition to the United States.

A lot of people wanted to talk to him. Besides Pennsylvania's, indictments for Hilton stacked up from New Jersey, Maryland and Virginia. The Coast Guard wanted him concerning allegations he'd bribed a seaman. More than two hundred witnesses were lined up to testify in what promised to be a lengthy and revealing trial.

Inquiring about his whereabouts lately, where he'd been, the *Philadelphia Inquirer* described Hilton as "full of swagger," boasting of traveling all over the world. Diplomatic complications with Canada over Hilton were only one international quandary area officials faced in early 1933. The French presented a stickier matter.

The Coast Guard became embroiled with France over the fate of the *Etchpatchis*, a seventy-five-foot rumrunner. A Coast Guard cutter rammed it in early February outside U.S. territorial limits. Actually, to make certain there was no misunderstanding, the cutter rammed *Etchi* twice.

The French Consul in Philadelphia received a formal complaint from *Etchi*'s master, Francois Riou, which was transmitted to the French embassy in Washington, the *Inquirer* reported on February 7. The Coast Guard asserted Riou's complaint was fabricated to avoid the real issue. His ship carried over one thousand cases of "choice" liquor.

One problem with Riou's story was Riou's history. He'd been banned from returning to the United States because of his involvement with Rum Row. In fact, American officials swore that *Etchi* was Riou's former rumrunner, the *Emma Helene*. Both captain and ship were tied to the Hilton Rum Ring.

Riou countered that he was transporting liquor from St. Pierre, French territory, to the Bahamas. He claimed he'd entered Delaware Bay breakwater to make repairs.

While French and American diplomats wrangled, eight of the fifty men indicted in the Hilton case entered guilty pleas, the *New York Times* reported, opening day of that trial. Fourteen of the fifty, including the "mastermind," remained fugitive. Hilton lingered in Montreal, fighting extradition to the United States.

Many involved with the ring were locally prominent, so considerable pressure was applied to federal prosecutors to refrain from publicly disclosing identities. It didn't work. Names appeared in newspapers.

One name that did not appear belonged to the mysterious "postmaster somewhere along the New Jersey coast," who enabled smugglers to land illegal goods with impunity. That was the only identifying information provided in the testimony of Francis Wills, undercover federal agent who obtained his information by tapping telephones at ring offices.

Wills was unable to name the postmaster or his location. His testimony was based upon transcripts of recorded conversations, including Hilton, about "delivery delays." The *Inquirer* published snippets of these conversations: "The postmaster is doing it. He said we'd better wait for a while," Hilton was recorded telling an associate. "He said it'll be all right [landing liquor] in a couple days and I'm going along with him."

"Everything's lined up. Sheriff. State troopers. Coast Guard."

A battery of fourteen defense attorneys led by Congressman Benjamin Gulder (Republican, PA) sought to discredit Wills's testimony, particularly the wiretap evidence, contending that government agents had obtained it by means of illegal entry, thus invalidating the search warrant and its use in court.

Wills testified that all the evidence used to bring down the ring was contained in two thousand transcribed pages of wiretaps. Cape May County was featured as a primary "drop" point for illegal liquor.

Stories piled up, layer upon layer. On February 14, the *New York Times* reported that seaman Samuel Coppens was paid $100 a week to advise smugglers of movements of Coast Guard vessels, facilitating the ring's coordination of cargo landings.

Hilton was recorded issuing instructions to "take $100 to William Burns on Corgie Street in Cape May." "Burns" was an alias Coppens used when dealing with the ring. He lived on Corgie Street. Coppens occupied the witness chair after lengthy Wills testimony. He identified a photo of the man in charge, the man who paid him—Frank Hilton.

The four-week trial ended on March 2, with ten members of the ring found guilty of conspiracy to violate Prohibition laws. The jury deliberated less than three hours. Those convicted—along with four others who'd pleaded guilty—were sentenced to the two-year maximum federal prison sentence. The rest who'd pleaded guilty were fined and released because they'd cooperated with prosecutors.

Defense attorneys scrambled to file appeals and motions for new trials. Special Attorney General Chet Keyes, lead prosecutor, advised the court he'd learned that while the trial proceeded, the ring's operations persisted.

Federal agents seized what the *Inquirer* described as a "field headquarters of south Jersey's largest rum ring."

Eight federal agents, backed by state police, raided a location near Margate, just north of Ocean City. They seized a radio station used to direct a mother ship and two couriers.

According to investigators, six speedboats connected with this operation had landed over seven thousand cases of liquor at points along Delaware Bay, Cape May and Wildwood.

And what of Hilton?

"He'll be brought back for trial soon," Keyes assured reporters. Unfortunately, Keyes spoke from Philadelphia while Hilton remained in Montreal. Outgoing president Herbert Hoover signed Hilton's extradition papers. The fugitive awaited a "final hearing" in Canada.

Since the conspiracy charge against Hilton wasn't considered an extraditable offense, the United States sought his return on the bribery charge involving Seaman Coppens.

"If Canada surrenders Hilton, he'll likely be tried in Trenton first [on the bribery charge]," Keyes explained. "Then here." That "if" remained a question mark.

The Coast Guard wasn't awaiting Hilton's return to resume the war against illegal booze. In mid-March, patrol boats ran a smuggler ashore at Sunset Beach, chasing their quarry five miles until it ran aground. Authorities seized 126 barrels of liquor. The crew leaped ashore, making good their escape.

Another trio of smugglers wasn't so lucky. The Coast Guard pursued them for an hour, capturing their vessel, the *Laura*, by firing a shell that crippled its propeller just off Brandywine Shoals.

The crewmen were arrested and their cargo of 300 cases of booze added to the growing government stockpile at Philadelphia Customs House. At Wildwood, the twin-screw fishing vessel *Julia Davis* sat at anchor, seized with 592 sacks of booze aboard, valued at $240,000. Attorney for the boat's owner, Tobias Johnson of Brooklyn, told the court the boat had been stolen and turned to a life of crime.

Wildwood's reorganized police didn't find much illegal booze in early 1933, but Acting Chief Mike Sheehan kept his troops busy ferreting out another vice that had grown in recent years.

Once again raiding at Otten's Harbor, police hit two "disorderly houses," apprehending several working girls who gave addresses in Gloucester City. Harry Kendella was charged as "leader of a vice ring." That charge was eventually dismissed, but officers did find a quantity of liquor, so they settled for possession charges.

Must have been a slow night at the house—no male patrons were apprehended.

***

After all the Philadelphia courtroom drama and international tap dancing, Canada refused to extradite Frank Hilton. Canadian court would not accept as evidence the testimony of Samuel Coppens, nor would that court allow wiretap evidence prosecutors submitted.

Hilton was released, free to live out his life, presumably in Canada. Less than two months later, he was dead.

Doctors in Montreal reported Hilton died in his apartment on June 25 from acute indigestion. He was forty-two years old.

The *Wildwood Leader* expanded on Hilton's story. He was born in Anglesea at First and Central Avenues. Second son of former mayor Augustus Hilton, his address for the 1930 census was given as 347 East Maple Avenue, Wildwood. His parents' address. Hilton had no college education and was unmarried. The census listed his profession as fisherman.

His funeral was held at his father's home. Hilton's pallbearers included Harry Tenenbaum, Wildwood city solicitor and frequent attorney for accused Volstead violators; C.A. Heil, Wildwood city clerk; and Bernard Maxwell, Wildwood Republican leader, who carried the coffin as well.

The *Leader* offered a brief summary of Hilton's career, calling it a "left-handed success story." Hilton began bootlegging early into Prohibition, the paper reported. Blessed with a thirsty local market and "agreeable public officials," Hilton leveraged his position as part of one of the area's largest fishing businesses, Consolidated Fisheries, using his connections to funnel liquor into the area via coastal and bayside Cape May County.

He scoffed at government efforts to extradite him and, while on the lam, enjoyed a lavish lifestyle in Montreal while treating himself to a first-class trip around the world. Ironically, Hilton was in financial straits at the time of the ring's collapse. He'd invested heavily in a "legitimate" enterprise, Suburban Title and Trust Company, under the name J. Frank Moore. When the Depression hit, as one trial witness expressed it, Hilton was "up to his knees" at the bank when it failed.

There was additional fallout from dismantling of Hilton's ring in the fall of 1933, when 150 people, including some of the "most socially prominent names of Philadelphia" were indicted by federal grand jury for their involvement with the ring's activities.

For probably the last time, a rum fleet gathered off New Jersey, more than twenty-five ships, the greatest armada since 1925.

This time, they anticipated Prohibition's repeal and a flood of demand for their legalized product. Authorities estimated that 300,000 gallons had been kept in storage at "rum bases," in anticipation of massive movement of liquor after repeal before imposition of a tariff on booze.

Also anticipating, officials had already initiated a "buy legal" campaign, encouraging liquor buyers to purchase "stamped" product, properly taxed. They suggested that buying unstamped liquor would be unpatriotic. Buying from the rum fleet would deprive the government of $50 million revenue.

After fourteen years, Prohibition had come full circle. Starting with an appeal to patriotism to stop drinking, it ended with an appeal to patriotism

Wildwood mayor Doris Bradway. *George F. Boyer Historical Museum.*

to drink only government sanctioned liquor. On December 5, Utah's ratification commission voted to ratify the Twenty-First Amendment, repealing the Eighteenth.

A week later, Wildwood City Hall was busy. City commission had set a $500 price for retail liquor licenses and would-be buyers lined up to get theirs. The first license went to Hugh McCardle. Thirteen others sold quickly, with more applications for commissioners to review.

Some of the names sounded familiar, belonging not to Leamings or Spicers or Hands but to former speakeasy operators like Turchi, Dauginais and Applegate.

"Price of a drink of whisky will be 25 cents for an ounce and a half," McCardle decreed, setting the going price for others to follow. Mayor Doris Bradway called upon Wildwood's newest businesses to help police eliminate the remaining speakeasies persisting in the resort. It was in their best interest to do just that.

***

Miss Hannah Ludlam Townsend passed away in March 1934, dying in the home in which she'd been born on October 18, 1842.

She was the oldest woman resident born in Cape May County. Her pedigree on her mother's side extended back to colonial times. An ancestor was the first white settler in the area, Joseph Ludlam. Her grandfather Henry fought in the Revolution. A great uncle built the Mainstay Inn, one of Cape May's first hotels.

Her father, William S. Townsend, former county freeholder, was scion of two venerable families, the Smiths and Townsends. The Townsend branch were Quakers arrived in the area in the late seventeenth century.

Hannah's dry sentiments ran in the family. William was a temperance man.

***

On April 18, Judge Henry Eldredge died at his home in West Cape May. A descendant of John Howland who came to the New World on the *Mayflower* and one of the area's first settlers, Eldredge was fifty-three years old.

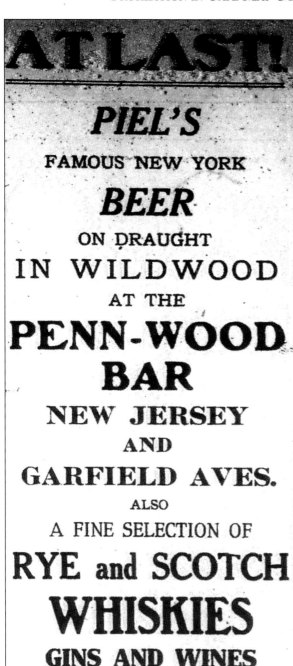

Newspaper ad announcing that beer is back. *From the* Cape May Gazette.

***

A full-page ad in the April 26 *Wildwood Journal Tribune* said it all:

"At Last"

Beneath the bold type ran advertising for Piel's Famous New York Beer, "now in Wildwood" at the Penn-Wood Bar. "Hugh McCardle, Proprietor."

No more qualifiers like "alleged" were required.

***

Shortly before Prohibition's repeal, Coast Guardsmen seized an International truck loaded with 150 cases of liquor at Dennis Creek.

Investigating the suspicious-looking truck, parked in a remote area near the bay, guardsmen were fired upon. The shooters fled, abandoning truck and cargo.

The truck's owner was identified as Benson's Service Station in Woodbine.

After Prohibition, Other Passings

What became of bootleggers after repeal? Some entered legitimate liquor businesses. Some went into organized crime. Some continued bootlegging.

"One of the most curious facts about post repeal was that the manufacture and smuggling of illicit liquor continued in great volume," Frederick Lewis Allen wrote in *Only Yesterday*.

That was due in part to the scarcity of liquor with American producers out of commission for so long. And it resulted from a desire to avoid paying federal and state taxes imposed on legal booze. The IRS continued seizing and destroying stills at a rate of fifteen thousand per year.

Just before the twenty-first amendment passed, FDR created the Federal Alcohol Control Administration to regulate the industry. States established their own regulatory agencies. Within two years after repeal, alcohol tax was generating 13 percent of government revenue.

People wanted to drink legally, but it was the Depression and money was tight. Between the limited supply of liquor and added costs imposed by taxation, drinkers sought less-expensive sources.

Two years after repeal, anywhere from 15 to 60 percent of the booze imbibed in America was bootleg. People were glad Prohibition was over. *Fortune* magazine surveys in 1937 showed 15.1 percent of men and 29.7 percent of women missed Prohibition.

In Woodbine, it didn't matter whether booze was legal or not. Woodbine was an unusual community for an area as deeply immersed in "traditional"

Christianity as Cape May County. Founded in 1891 by trustees of the Baron de Hirsch Fund as a Jewish farming colony, by 1900, Woodbine claimed 1,400 residents. The $24 million fund was created to address the needs of Jewish immigrants to help Americanize and make them self-sufficient citizens.

The Baron de Hirsch Agricultural School of Woodbine taught young Jewish men practical farming.

But Woodbine didn't limit itself to farming. The town boasted factories, making clothing and baskets and two machine shops.

The original town consisted of 5,300 acres with 65 farmhouses and 150 town homes, along with a bath house, hotel and synagogue. The first refugees cleared land

Baron de Hirsch. *Sam Azeez Museum of Woodbine Heritage.*

and built homesteads, each having fifteen acres. Each family was provided a horse, material to build a barn, cow, twenty-five chickens, tools and seeds to go with the land.

Farmers grew fruit, vegetables, corn, peas and cereal grains. They also grew grapes. According to Joseph Brandeis in his *Immigrants to Freedom*, some of the grape crop went to Vineland, where a dentist named Welch invented a new product, grape juice.

The rest of the grapes were used to make wine.

Its off-the-beaten-track location, convenient to seashore resorts, combined with a do-it-yourself individualism to make Woodbine an ideal place for moonshining to flourish during Prohibition. From the start of the dry years, Woodbine was a hotbed of home-based brewing and distilling. The area received almost as much attention from law enforcement as the Wildwoods.

Typical swampy area near Belleplain. *Dennis Township Museum.*

Even after repeal, the Woodbine area continued to go its own way when it came to laws governing alcohol.

The *Gazette* headline read "Coast Guard to Halt Smuggling along the Bay." With the repeal of Prohibition, the Coast Guard marshalled its forces to specific areas where smuggling persisted in the county, especially West Creek in Dennis Township.

Seamen searched trucks for everything from heroin to illegal aliens, but particularly, untaxed booze.

Lieutenant R.L. Burke, in charge at the air station at Cape May, linked his forces with customs agents in an effort to root out illegal "contraband." A month into their campaign, papers across the country carried reports of a raid on a still that resulted in the shooting death of Herman Benson, Woodbine's volunteer fire chief.

Aerial view of West Creek looking toward Delaware Bay. *Dennis Township Museum.*

Coast Guard officials stated that Benson, armed with several weapons, threatened raiders when they seized the still. A few days before the encounter, air surveillance had spotted the still located in woods near Woodbine.

Four raiders approached the site. While one returned to the main road to call for help, Benson appeared, armed with a sawed-off shotgun and .45-caliber pistol. He disarmed two of the three remaining seamen, marching them at gunpoint toward the third, Harry Milliken. Benson confronted Milliken. The seaman fired his submachine gun, wounding Benson.

Benson was taken to the hospital, where he died of five gunshot wounds, three to the abdomen, two to the head. Louis Benson, the deceased's brother and former Woodbine police chief, was held along with two other men as operators of the still.

"We saw a truck drive deep into the woods," Burke said. "We followed and found four men watching a gigantic still. We were as surprised as they were."

Three of the four moonshiners fled while fire was exchanged. After waiting several hours, a truck approached the site. Louis Benson was driving along with Louis Kaufman of Philadelphia. The pair was arrested.

The still, concealed inside a burlap tent, was operating when raiders arrived. They found four vats filled with mash and five thousand gallons of finished alcohol in large drums.

Herman Benson was allegedly under the influence when he arrived on the scene. "I've got you covered," he shouted. The seamen dropped their weapons. At this point, Milliken, appeared and "got the drop" on Benson.

"Now I've got you covered." he reportedly said.

Benson whirled about to face Milliken, brandishing weapons. Did he fire? Milliken took no chances.

This was not the Bensons' first clash with the Coast Guard over a two-year period. Herman Benson had been arrested for attacking seaman Edward Jarvis, who was investigating illegal liquor smuggling in the area. Benson was out on bail awaiting trial for that incident when the shooting occurred.

Authorities described Herman Benson as a "notorious bootlegger" who fancied himself a tough guy. His encounter with Jarvis had ended with Benson "beating" the seaman. Benson claimed Jarvis tried to "shake me down" with Jarvis countering that Benson's truck smelled of liquor, and when he attempted to search the vehicle, Benson attacked him, threatening his life.

The Bensons had other encounters with the Coast Guard. A boat slipping past surveillance had managed to land booze that authorities traced to another farm outside Woodbine. This farm belonged to Jacob, another of the Benson brothers. Authorities seized several hundred gallons of liquor.

Coincidentally, that raid had also been led by Burke.

And two years earlier, the Benson gang had a run-in with Coast Guard near Corson's Inlet when warrant officer Christopher Bentham came upon eleven men unloading smuggled liquor. Before being knocked unconscious, Bentham memorized the license plate of the escape vehicle. Seven men were subsequently arrested.

Ironically, had the shooting not occurred, Benson would have been arrested anyway. John Pennington, state head of the Federal Alcohol Tax Unit, indicated that a warrant "was about to be executed for Benson's failure to report purchases of molasses and sugar for distillery purposes."

Then came the trials. Louis was tried for operating the fifty-thousand-gallon capacity still. He produced character witnesses from Woodbine who testified that his "reputation was very good," the *Daily Journal* reported.

Not good enough apparently. He was found guilty on October 23, sentenced to five months' jail and fined $500.

The following July, brother Jacob was indicted for concealing eight hundred gallons of untaxed liquor.

In its effort to eradicate illegal booze, the government began using a new tactic in late 1935. It indicted suppliers of materials used for making liquor. Ten men, several identified as "dealers in sugar and molasses," were charged with supplying the Benson still, listed as operating under (Herman) Benson Trucking Company, with raw materials, "knowing the device was being operated contrary to law."

Louis Benson's name headed that list. Another, Abe Katz, had been indicted with the Bensons involved in the Jarvis incident. Four were eventually jailed following trial in Camden. Katz was released. Benson was given probation in this instance.

The IRS wanted a piece of Jacob Benson too. In 1937, he was convicted of concealing untaxed liquor, the *Leader* reported.

With 820 gallons seized at a price of $7 per gallon, the taxable value of the liquor figured to $5,740.

To complicate Benson's legal situation further, federal agents revealed that a building on the Benson farm had been used as a "drop" for smugglers bringing illegal liquor from boats landing it at West Creek. Louis Benson was indicted again.

The old saying about death and taxes applied in spades to Herman Benson, who allegedly failed to file returns on $40,449 between 1932 and 1934.

At least, that's what his widow's lawyer told the U.S. Board of Tax Appeals in Eva Benson's petition on tax delinquency. The lawyer indicated the money was earned by the Benson Trucking Company, not by the man, and asked that "liens be lifted against personal bank accounts with charges dropped so the estate could be settled."

***

In May 1935, the Coast Guard once again captured the *Etchi*. It was disguised as a fishing vessel, captained by Francoise Riou, who gave his address as St. Pierre. Five French citizens were arrested, and two thousand cases of liquor, valued at $50,000, were seized.

This time, there was no question of territorial waters. The law caught *Etchi* right off Cape May Point. But as in their previous encounter, the schooner played coy with pursuers and attempted to flee. The cutter fired on it, forcing *Etchi* to surrender.

This was the fourth time the ship had been seized. Riou had managed its release on the last occasion, claiming he'd been flying distress signals when the Coast Guard took the ship. This time, authorities accepted no excuses.

Etchi was towed to sea off southern New Jersey and dynamited. Its remains joined an underwater marine sanctuary artificial reef system.

***

John Adams, former Methodist pastor in Ocean City and terror of speakeasies and politicians he considered soft on wets, passed away quietly after a brief illness, the *Leader* reported on April 4, 1935.

Adams was a peculiar combination of tenacity and bombast. Adams wore a cleric's collar but reveled in making the "collars" of the lawman. He belonged to a unique breed of men that emerged nationwide during the Volstead era, earning a title, bestowed seriously and in jest.

The Raiding Parson was seventy-two.

***

The *Camden Courier Post* reported the return of King Nummy's ghost to an island in Hereford Inlet, one of Nummy's many purported burial spots. At the time of writing, the island was home to the "long-abandoned Hereford Inlet Fishing Club."

According to nearby residents of Anglesea, Nummy's nightly appearances were accompanied by beating tom-toms, "calling the Lenape tribe to reclaim what was once theirs." According to historian Lewis Townsend Stevens, the Lenape "mysteriously disappeared from this area after the death of Nummy and his burial on this island."

Or were these nightly visitations of a less spectral nature? Instead of tom-toms, the sputterings of boat engines in the night. Rumrunners seeking a secluded dumping spot for liquid goods after a rough haul from Rum Row through the treacherous Hereford

The *Post* offered no opinion.

Local anglers, returning from the fishing grounds, reported phosphorescent glows moving through the old clubhouse at midnight. "Hovers over Nummy's grave then floats through the building," Pete Petersen told the paper.

Petersen did more than observe. The intrepid local sailed his skiff out to the island to investigate.

What did he find?

No booze. No evidence of tribal gatherings. In fact, sands around the clubhouse remained perfectly undisturbed. Nary a footprint. But inside…

A fresh trail through accumulated dust made by the soft tread of an Indian moccasin led all through the building until it stopped abruptly and vanished.

Some fishermen avoided the island, fearing interference of spirits in their already dangerous occupation. Others steered clear from the less metaphysical fear of facing a bootlegger's revolver.

**

I tried to avoid mentioning "big names" from the era because I didn't want to distract from the role Prohibition played in Cape May County.

But an April 1, 1939 *New York Times* article suggests the county played a significant role in the machinations of organized crime during the era.

The scene was Johnny Torrio's tax evasion trial. A "surprise" witness appeared to testify for the prosecution.

Captain Bert Errickson, described by the paper as "a balding and placid Scandinavian fishing boat captain and rumrunner," told the court how the "big operation" brought millions of dollars in illegal liquor into the country.

Through Wildwood.

Bert detailed costs like an accountant. How much booze cost in Canada. How much to transport it to mother ships. Loading costs. Shipping costs. Supplies. Fuel. He dwelled at length on costs incurred for breakage. Costs incurred by "little guys" like himself.

Prices for product. Cheap scotch? A case went for eight bucks. Fishing boats typically charged so much a case to transport it. Add another dollar a case to unload it once landed. Another buck if you wanted it loaded on the truck. Errickson knew prices of various liquors right down to what the guy on the street paid for his taste.

He detailed procedures. Where the booze was produced. Where it was shipped from. How it was transferred to landing craft.

Then he named names.

He'd met Torrio a number of times. He also recalled Al Lillien, who operated a fleet of trucks out of Atlantic Highlands, headquartered at a mansion once owned by Oscar Hammerstein.

Johnny Torrio mug shot. *Mark Herron.*

He mentioned Johnny Campbell, known as King of the Atlantic City bootleggers. In the calm tones of a man used to braving the stormy North Atlantic, he named them all. King Solomon from Boston. Joe Adonis from Brooklyn.

He admitted under cross-examination that he'd never seen Torrio on a rum boat or in Wildwood at meetings of the "association," the word Errickson used to describe the rumrunners and "syndicate men" who periodically gathered at local speakeasies to decide how to control liquor volumes, what prices to charge and related matters of business.

Errickson also admitted he was a convicted rumrunner, awaiting sentencing for a guilty plea in a liquor case. But the damage was done. Courtroom observers sensed the tension. They felt violent rage boiling around the defense table with each response the Wildwood fisherman offered.

In the end, the soft-spoken salt splashed sleepy Cape May County prominently across the Prohibition map. Big time.

Was there ever any doubt?

Bibliography

Books

Allen, Everett. *Black Ships*. Carlisle, MA: Commonwealth Editions, 2015.

Allen, Frederick Lewis. *Only Yesterday*. New York: Harper & Row, 1931.

Behr, Edward. *Prohibition*. New York: Arcade Publishing, 1996.

Berkey, Joan, and Joseph E. Salvatore. *US Coast Guard Training Center at Cape May*. Charleston, SC: Arcadia Publishing, 2012.

Boyer, George F. *Wildwood, Middle of the Island*. Egg Harbor City, NJ: Laureate Press, 1976.

Boyer, George F., and J. Pearson Cunningham. *Cape May County Story*. Egg Harbor City, NJ: Laureate Press, 1975.

Burcher, Joseph. *Remembering South Cape May*. Charleston, SC: The History Press, 2010.

Burnham, John. *Bad Habits*. New York: New York University Press, 1993.

Burningham, Lucy. *My Beer Year*. Boulder, CO: Roost Books, 2016.

Burns, Eric. *1920: The Year that Made the Decade Roar*. New York: Pegasus Books, 2015.

———. *Spirits of America*. Philadelphia: Temple University Publishing, 2004.

Cheever, Susan. *Drinking in America*. New York: Twelve, 2016.

Cooper, Alfred. *My Traditions and Memories, 1859–1938*. Cape May Court House, NJ: Gazette Print Shop, 1938.

Cope, Nathan. *The Story of Cape May County Trains and Trolleys*. Mile Beach Electric Railway Company, 1993.

Dorwart, Jeffery M. *Cape May County, New Jersey: The Making of an American Resort Community*. Camden, NJ: Rutgers University Press, 1992.

Francis, David W., Diane Demali Francis and Robert J. Scully. *Wildwood by the Sea*. Fairview Park, OH: Amusement Park Books, 1998.

Kallen, Stuart A., ed. *The Roaring Twenties*. San Diego: Greenhaven Press, 2002.

Kerr, K. Austin. *Organized for Prohibition: A New History of the Anti-Saloon League*. New Haven, CT: Yale University Press, 1985.

Kobler, John. *Ardent Spirits*. Boston: Da Capo Press, 1993.

Koedel, R. Craig. *South Jersey Heritage: Social, Economic, and Cultural History*. Washington, D.C.: University Press of America, 1979. http://westjersey.org/sjh/sjh_title.htm.

Kyvig, David. *Daily Life in the United States: 1920–1940*. Chicago: Ivan R. Dee, 2002.

———. *Repealing National Prohibition*. Kent, OH: Kent University Press, 2000.

McCutheon, Marc. *Writer's Guide to Everyday Life from Prohibition through World War II*. Cincinnati, OH: Writer's Digest Books, 1995.

Okrent, Daniel. *Last Call: The Rise and Fall of Prohibition*. New York: Scribner, 2010.

Reeves, Ira L. *Ol' Rum River*. Chicago: Thomas S. Rockwell Company, 1931.

Richey, Russell E., Jean Miller Schmidt, Kenneth E. Rowe. *American Methodism*. Abingdon Press, 2010.

Rorabaugh, W.J. *The Alcoholic Republic: An American Tradition*. New York: Oxford University Press, 1981.

———. *Prohibition: A Concise History*. New York: Oxford University Press, 2018.

Sann, Paul. *The Lawless Decade*. Mineola, NY: Dover Publications, 1957.

Sea Isle City Historical Society. *Memories of Days Gone by in Sea Isle City*. Sea Isle City, NJ: Sea Isle Historical Society, 1990.

Slavicek, Louise Chipley. *The Prohibition Era*. New York: Chelsea House Publications, 2008.

Smith, Gregg. *Beer: A History of Suds and Civilization from Mesopotamia to Microbreweries*. New York: Avon Books, 1995.

Sullivan, Audrey, Doris Young. *A Time to Remember: A History of New Jersey Methodists' First Camp Meeting, South Seaville, New Jersey, 1864–1988*. South Seaville, NJ: South Seaville Camp Meeting Association Inc., 1988.

Van de Water, Frederic. *The Real McCoy*. Mystic, CT: Flat Hammock Press, 2007.

Waters, Harold. *Smugglers of Spirits: Prohibition and the Coast Guard Patrol*. East Sussex, UK: Hasting House Press, 1971.

NEWSPAPERS

Allentown Morning Call
Asbury Park Press
Baltimore Evening Sun
Cape May County Gazette
Cape May County Times
Cape May Star and Wave
Central New Jersey Home News
Delaware County Daily Times
Des Moines Register
Five Mile Beach Journal
Harrisburg Evening News
Harrisburg Telegraph
New York Times
Ocean City Sentinel
Philadelphia Inquirer
Philadelphia Public Ledger
Pittsburgh Post Gazette
Sayre Evening Times
Scranton Republican
Trenton Times
Vineland Daily Journal
Wildwood Leader
Wildwood Tribune Journal
Wilkes-Barre Evening News
Wilkes-Barre Record
Wilmington Evening Journal
Wilmington Morning News

ARTICLES/PERIODICALS

Cape May County Gazette. "In Another Time: Reforms, Suffrage, and High Stakes Politics a Century Ago." May 31, 2012.

Cape May County Historical and Genealogical Society Magazine, various years.

Leader. "In Another Time: Fishing Has Always Been Dangerous Work." June 15, 2013.

Lerner, Michael. "Going Dry." *Humanities Magazine* 32, no. 5 (September/October 2011).

McGrew, Jane Lang. "History of Alcohol Prohibition." Paper presented to National Commission on Drug and Alcohol Abuse. Located online at www.druglibrary.org.

State University of New York Press. "The Friedman Legacy." 2013.

———. "Rum Row." 2013.

About the Author

Raymond Rebmann is retired after thirty years with the New Jersey Department of Labor and now works as a curator for the Old School House Museum in Dennisville, New Jersey. A reporter and columnist for twenty years for the *Cape May County Herald* newspaper, he has also authored several books, including *Dennis Township* (Arcadia), *How Can You Give Up that Adorable Puppy* (Unlimited Publishing) and *Jersey Devil, Cursed Unfortunate* (MuseItUp). His children grown and moved on, he lives in a log cabin in the woods of South Seaville with his wife, dog, cat and horse. In addition to writing, beach combing and gardening, he is a determined home brewer with an experimental bent.

Visit us at
www.historypress.com